MW01109290

The Great Pastamaker Cookbook

*An exciting collection
of fresh, healthy and
easy-to-make recipes*

Copyright © 2013 by KitchenAdvance.
All rights reserved. No portion of this book may be
reproduced by any means without permission in
writing from the publisher.

Printed in the United States of America.

ISBN: 978-1-938653-16-2

TABLE OF CONTENTS

CHAPTER 4

CHAPTER 5

TABLE OF CONTENTS

CHAPTER 12

CHAPTER 13

CHAPTER 14

CHAPTER 15

Introduction

Chapter 1

Nobody knows when the first pasta was made, but it is certainly one of the world's oldest foods. The Chinese developed their noodles as early as 5000 B.C., and later introduced them into Japan through Korea.   Early East European nomads carried a type of dried dough that was grated into boiling goats milk.   In ancient Greece and Rome, cooks created a pasta known as laganon or laganum, similar to today's tagliatelle. And the early Arab world invented its own version of pasta, called couscous.

Some say that Marco Polo brought the first pasta to Europe, but in fact pasta had become common throughout Europe, Asia, the Middle East and North Africa, by the middle ages.   Five hundred years later Thomas Jefferson earned his place in culinary history when he visited Naples, Italy, and had four crates of "maccarony" shipped home.

In Italian, pasta means "paste", and that's exactly what it is: a mixture of ground grain and liquid. But the wide variety of forms makes this simple description truly inadequate. For example, hard durum wheat semolina, a glutinous flour that makes a stiff dough, can be mixed with water to produce couscous and the many versions of dried Italian pasta. And fresh Italian pasta, a combination of eggs and bread flour yields golden noodles. Asians use bleached and whole-wheat flours as well as rice, buckwheat, potato, mung bean, soybean, yam, pea, taro, tapioca, and even acorn flours to make their noodles. In India, cooks prepare a dish from chick pea flour, which they call besan, and noodles named phaluda from corn starch. Germans, Poles, and other Central Europeans create various egg noodles and dumplings from soft wheat flour. Over time, Americans have added their own innovations to these.

Noodle makers around the world knead, roll, tear, cut and twist dough into forms as plain as flat and rectangular and as complicated as cappelletti. Some doughs are flavored with puréed vegetables, exotic spices and even chocolate. Pasta is boiled, steamed, poached, baked or fried and served either hot or cold. Noodles can be stuffed and layered with meat, fish, fowl, vegetables, cheese and herbs. The choice of toppings includes sweet or spicy sauces of every imaginable description, including plain butter, pureed frog's legs, sesame sauce and squid ink.

Pasta is really very nutritious, and it doesn't have to be fattening. Pasta is bulky, so it fills you up quickly without loading you down with calories. One cup or about 5-ounces, contains just over 200 calories, compared with 550 for five ounces of steak. High in complex carbohydrates and low in fat, a typical serving of pasta offers 10 to 30 percent of the minimum daily requirements of several important vitamins and minerals. It also provides a surprising amount of protein. Ordinary pasta contains almost 10 grams of protein in a l-cup serving, while ""high protein"" pasta has about 15 grams. And whole-wheat pasta is high in dietary fiber.

If you're concerned about cholesterol, use vegetable toppings and sauces that contain no dietary cholesterol. Add fresh chopped tomatoes and, minced chives, or liven up canned tomatoes with sliced mushrooms and a splash of red wine. Since you can make it so many ways, pasta is for everyone!

Making Pasta

Chapter 2

Each recipe serves 4 to 6 people
unless otherwise indicated.

——— —— —— ——

Most of the recipes in this book
call for a full load of fresh pasta dough
made into a specific pasta shape using
the Automatic Pasta Maker.

——— —— —— ——

All of the pasta dough recipes can be
mixed and rolled by hand and many of
the shapes can be cut by hand if you
don't have a machine.

——— —— —— ——

You may substitute
16 ounces of dried pasta
for a full load of fresh pasta.

MAKING PASTA

In addition to the basic pasta dough recipe in your Automatic Pasta Maker Instruction Booklet, you will be able to make all the fresh pastas in this book with the following pasta dough recipes. Use the pasta measuring cup that comes with the Automatic Pasta Maker to measure your flour. Mix remaining ingredients as directed in the pasta maker instruction booklet. **Remember, these recipes are for a full load of pasta and all of the recommendations in the booklet for making a basic pasta dough apply to the different pasta recipes below.**

If you are not using the Automatic Pasta Machine, substitute 4 cups of flour for 2 pasta measuring cups. These pasta dough recipes can be mixed and kneaded by hand on a floured board, then rolled and stretched out with a floured rolling pin until almost transparently thin. Let sheets of rolled pasta rest for 15 minutes. Using a very sharp knife, you can cut rolled pasta sheets into wide noodles from 1/8" for tagliarini to 3/4" for pappardelle. Lasagna, cannelloni, bowties, butterflies, and other fancy shapes can be cut from sheets using the directions following the pasta recipes.

TRADITIONAL PASTA ALL'UOVO

2 pasta measuring cups all purpose flour
5 medium eggs
1/2 teaspoon salt (optional)
1-1/4 tablespoons olive oil

17

EGGLESS PASTA

*2 pasta measuring cups all purpose **or** special
mix semolina flour **or** 1 each pasta measuring
cup of all purpose and semolina flour
1/2 teaspoon salt (optional)
1/2 to 3/4 cup water
4 tablespoons olive oil*

WHOLE WHEAT PASTA

*1 pasta measuring cup all purpose flour **and**
1 pasta measuring cup of whole wheat flour
2 eggs
1 tablespoon olive oil
1/2 to 3/4 cup water
1/2 teaspoon salt (optional)*

BUCKWHEAT PASTA

*1 pasta measuring cup all purpose flour **and**
1 pasta measuring cup of buckwheat flour
4 eggs
1 tablespoon olive oil
1/2 teaspoon salt (optional)*

To make eggless Japanese buckwheat noodles, or
soba, substitute about 3/4 to 1 cup of water for the
eggs.

JAPANESE UDON

2 pasta measuring cups all purpose flour
1/2 to 1 teaspoon salt
3/4 to 1 cup water

Use the oriental noodle or vermicelli die to extrude pasta dough. If making by hand, knead the dough for 10 minutes and allow to rest for about an hour. Roll the dough into 1/8 inch thick sheets on a floured board and cut into 1/4 inch-wide noodles.

WON TON DOUGH

1-1/2 pasta measuring cups all purpose flour
1/2 pasta measuring cup cornstarch
1/2 teaspoon salt
2 eggs
2/3 cup water

Make sheets for *won ton* skins, egg rolls or *dim sum* using the instructions for filled pasta in the Making Pasta chapter. If making by hand, mix ingredients and knead the dough for 10 minutes. Cut dough in half, wrap both portions in plastic wrap, and let rest for about 15 to 30 minutes. Keep the rolled dough in a square shape then trim edges. Use a straightedge to cut squares for *won tons* or a plain round cookie cutter for various *dim sum* such as dumplings or potstickers.

CHINESE EGG NOODLES

2 pasta measuring cups all purpose flour
1/2 to 1 teaspoon salt
3 eggs
1/2 cup water
1/4 teaspoon sesame oil

Use the oriental noodle die to extrude pasta dough or the manicotti die to make sheets for *won ton* skins, egg rolls, or *dim sum* (dumplings or pot-stickers) using the directions for filled pasta shapes in the Making Pasta chapter. If making by hand, mix flour, eggs, and water and knead the dough for 10 minutes. Form into a smooth ball and rub the sesame oil over the surface. Let it rest for about an hour. Roll the dough into 1/16 to 1/8 inch thick sheets on a floured board and cut into 1/16 to 1/8 inch-wide noodles about 8 to 10 inches long.

Try adding about 3 tablespoons of sesame paste, chopped fresh coriander, crushed ginger, or chili pepper pulp to the eggs and reduce the amount of water slightly.

CUT & FILLED PASTA

In addition to the Automatic Pasta Machine and the Pasta Machine Accessory Kit, we recommend that you have the following:

1. A large cutting board or large, smooth work surface.
2. A large, sharp knife.
3. A long rolling pin.
4. A fluted pastry wheel.
5. A 2-inch and a 3-inch diameter circle cookie cutter plus other cookie and aspic cutters in a variety of shapes and sizes.
6. A metal straightedge or long ruler.

THE BASIC PASTA SHEET

The Manicotti die from the Pasta Machine Accessory Kit is the basis for making most cut and filled pasta shapes. Use the following technique for making the basic pasta sheets.

First, make a full load of your favorite pasta dough. Then use the manicotti to extrude tubes about 10" long. With a scissors, cut the tube open lengthwise and spread it flat on a lightly floured work surface.

Next, use a floured rolling pin to roll out the sheets of pasta even thinner to about a 1/16" thickness. Left over trimmings can either be put back into the machine and extruded again or formed into a dough ball and rolled out again by hand. If returned to the machine, you may need to add a little water to maintain proper extrusion consistency. Continue this process until you have made the entire load of pasta into the shape needed for the type of cut or filled pasta you are making.

CUTTING PASTA SHAPES

Lasagne or Cannelloni

Prepare filling and set aside. Make basic pasta sheets. Cut shapes for lasagne to fit your dish or cut 5 x 4-inch rectangles for cannelloni. The shapes can then be cooked then used to layer lasagne or roll around filling before baking.

NOTE: You can use manicotti tubes and lasagne noodles just as they are extruded from their individual dies. Remember the only real difference between maniciotti and cannelloni is that the ends of manicotti are sealed. We feel using the basic pasta sheet for cutting shapes is easier and gives a better result for both manicotti and cannelloni.

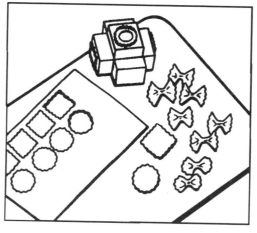

Butterflies and Bowties

Both butterflies and bowties can be made from the basic rolled pasta sheet. Use the 4-way Ravioli Cutter to make circles or squares. Then just pinch gently together in the center.

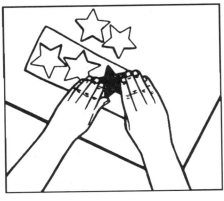

Using Cookie Cutter

You can use a variety of cookie and aspic cutters to make any kind of pasta shape from the basic rolled pasta sheet. With a little imagination, these unusual shapes can be used in almost any recipe.

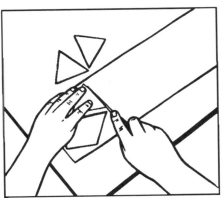

Using a Pattern

If you don't have a cutter the size and shape you desire, cut one out of clean, thin cardboard, lightly flour it, and use it as a template for cutting shapes.

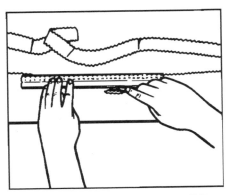

Cutting Strips

You can also make noodles with a fluted edge in any width by running a pastry wheel against the edge of a ruler as illustrated.

MAKING FILLED PASTA

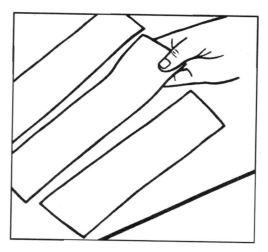

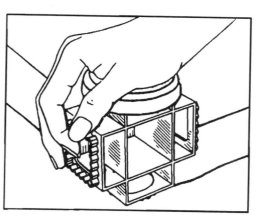

Small Ravioli Using the 4-Way Cutter

Prepare the filling and set aside. Make a full load of pasta dough and extrude into 8-inch long lasagne noodles using the lasagne die. Lay noodles on a lightly floured work surface and roll to about a 1/16" thickness. Now lay out a noodle and place 1/4 teaspoon of filling in the center of the noodle at about 1-inch intervals. Next, take another noodle strip, cover the filling, and cut with the 4-Way Ravioli Cutter as illustrated.

NOTE: To make sure raviolis and other stuffed pasta shapes stick together, brush exposed edges with beaten egg before cutting or pinching together. Also don't overstuff your shapes, they'll stay together better and look better when they're cooked.

24

Large Ravioli and Won Tons

Make filling and set aside. To make larger shapes, make a full load of pasta dough using the basic pasta sheet method. Make your pasta strips wider so you can spoon on more filling (use 1/2 teaspoon at 2-inch intervals). Lay a second sheet over the top. Press down firmly between the mounds of filling, and cut with a fluted pastry wheel as illustrated. Spread ravioli out on a dry towel to dry for about 30 minutes, turning over after 15 minutes. Be sure to keep them separated so they don't stick together.

NOTE: Round or semi-circular ravioli, called agnolotti, is made by cutting circles from the filled sheets of pasta. Be creative and cut triangles and other unusual shapes.

Half-Moon Ravioli and Dim Sum

Make filling and set aside. Make a full load of pasta dough using the basic pasta sheet method. Cut 2-inch diameter circles. Place a pea-size mound of filling in the center. Fold over one side of the circle and press edges firmly together.

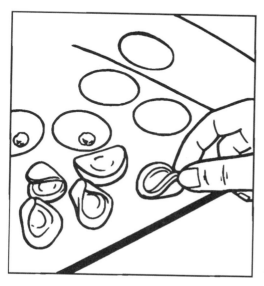

Tortellini

Use the same method as for half-moon ravioli, except place the filling slightly to one side of the middle. Fold over one side of circle so that it falls just short of the other side. Press edges firmly together. Curve the semi-circle around and pinch the edges together as illustrated.

Cappelletti

Use the same method as for Half-moon ravioli, except cut 2-inch squares instead of circles. Put filling in center of square. Fold in half diagonally to form a triangle, leaving a slight overlap between edges. Press edges together then wrap the long side of the triangle around your finger until the ends overlap. Press ends together firmly with the points of the triangle upright as illustrated.

NOTE: Allow half-moon ravioli, tortellini and cappelletti to dry as instructed for ravioli.

27

FLAVORED PASTAS

Following are some great ways to make pasta look and taste more interesting. By adding brightly colored and flavored ingredients you can create an entirely different look and flavor to your favorite pastas.

TOMATO PASTA

Add 4 tablespoons of tomato paste to the beaten egg or water from any pasta recipe. The bright orange hue is a nice contrast to white sauces.

SAFFRON PASTA

Just a dash of saffron gives pasta a warm yellow glow that's the perfect compliment to red or green vegetables. Simply sift a pinch or two of saffron into the flour before combining it with the other ingredients.

BEET PASTA

In a food processor or blender, pureé 1/2 cup of cooked beets. Press pureé through a strainer (this eliminates dark speckles). Add the beet puree to the egg or eggs and beat. Adjust the oil and water accordingly. Do not use canned or preserved beets.

CARROT PASTA

Omit half the oil and all of the water and add 2 tablespoons of carrot juice to the eggs. Pure carrot juice is available from natural food stores and delicatessens.

HERB PASTA

Add 4 tablespoons chopped mixed fresh herbs to flour. Suitable herbs include parsley, thyme, sage, tarragon, chives, chervil, marjoram and fennel. Use two or three different herbs, but be sure to balance the delicate herbs against the stronger ones by using less of the latter.

OLIVE PASTA

Add 1/2 cup of finely chopped black olives to the flour.

SPINACH PASTA

Wash and trim 1/2 pound of spinach. Cook over high heat for 5 minutes, shaking the pan often. Place the spinach in a strainer over a bowl. Press and squeeze juice from the spinach. Add 1/3 cup of spinach juice to pasta and adjust oil and water.

CHILI PASTA

Add 2 teaspoons cayenne pepper and 1 tablespoon hot chili oil to egg, and adjust oil and water.

COOKING PASTA

Pasta should be cooked in lots of boiling water. Although you might do with less water than what is recommended, which usually means using a stock pot or large kettle, you'll at least need a large pot which holds 4 to 4-1/2 quarts for cooking one full load of fresh pasta. You can also use a stock pot or large pressure cooker without the lid.

Fill the pot to three-quarters of its capacity. Add salt and bring the water to a boil. Adding a little oil to the water helps to prevent it from frothing on the surface and boiling over rapidly. Cooking in too little water will cause the noodles to stick together regardless of how much oil you may add to the water. When the water has reached a rolling boil, add the pasta, a little at a time, then stir it slightly and let the water return to a boil. Be ready to reduce the heat, to prevent it from boiling over.

Cook for about 3 minutes for noodles and other types of unfilled pasta. Filled pasta requires more cooking time for the filling to cook through. Dried pasta takes between 7 and 12 minutes. Time your sauce so that it is ready when the pasta finishes cooking. The pasta will become soft and gluey while waiting. Rinse pasta after draining only if it is to be used in a salad, then refrigerate.

DONENESS

When cooked, the pasta should be firm yet tender, or *al dente* (literally "to the tooth.") but not soft or sticky. When you cook pasta too long, it

30

absorbs too much cooking liquid. As a result, when sauce is added, the dish can become weepy or watery. Pasta that is still a little firm is more likely to absorb some of the liquid from the sauce, thus preventing a soggy finished dish. And if you're planning to further cook the pasta, such as in a dish of baked Lasagne, make sure the pasta is even a little firmer.

When the pasta is done, test it by cutting a piece with a fork, or taking a bite. The pasta will have only a slight bit of uncooked core, when it is al dente. Drain the cooked pasta at once, pouring it into a large strainer. Shake the strainer over the sink, then tip the pasta into a hot bowl and add the dressing or sauce. Serve at once.

CHILLING PREPARED PASTA

Dust the pasta with plenty of flour and place it in a large airtight container in the refrigerator. Cook within 2 days of making or freeze promptly. The unrolled dough may be wrapped and chilled for 1 to 2 days.

FREEZING PASTA

Uncooked fresh pasta freezes very well but it is best to make noodles or shapes first. Separate layers of pasta with freezer film or foil. Flour noodles well and pack them loosely in plastic bags, then lay them out flat for freezing. Do not thaw frozen pasta before cooking. Simply add it to boiling water and cook just like fresh pasta. Noodles and most other shapes take about the same time to cook as unfrozen pasta, once the water has come to a boil again. Frozen filled pasta requires extra cooking time to allow the filling to thaw and cook properly. Cooked lasagne and cannelloni or similar layered pasta dishes freeze well, but cooked shapes and noodles tend to have an inferior texture if frozen after cooking.

LASAGNE TIPS

For entertaining, or when time is tight, assemble the lasagne the night before. Cover and chill it. Then just add 5 to 10 minutes to the baking time. Or warm it a little by microwaving for a few minutes while your oven preheats.

You can also freeze unbaked lasagne by double-wrapping it and storing it in a freezer bag. It makes a great emergency meal for surprise guests. Put it right into the oven still frozen. Just cover it with foil and allow it to bake slowly. Baked or unbaked, it is good to slice individual portions before freezing. This makes it easy for your family to reheat single portions in the oven or microwave for quick dinners and snacks.

MAKING BREADSTICKS

CHEESE AND HERB STICKS

1-1/2 cups all-purpose flour
2 tablespoons Parmesan cheese, freshly grated
1/2 cup butter or margarine
1/2 teaspoon garlic powder
1/2 teaspoon onion powder
1 teaspoon Italian seasoning
1 cup sharp cheddar cheese, freshly grated
2 tablespoons cold water

Preheat oven to 375° F. In a small bowl thoroughly blend garlic powder, onion powder, and Italian seasoning with the butter. Add flour, Parmesan cheese and butter mixture to Pasta Machine and mix. Add cheddar, mix again and add the water. Continue mixing until dough forms pea-sized lumps of dough. (Refer to your Pasta Maker instruction booklet if you need to adjust for proper extrusion.) Using the bread stick die, extrude bread sticks to desired length and lay them on a non-stick baking sheet about 1 inch apart. Cook for 8 to 10 minutes or until golden brown. Remove from oven and allow to cool slightly before serving.

Tip: When making breadsticks, tilt Pasta Machine forward over the edge of the counter and allow the breadsticks to extrude downward. Pinch them off with your fingers when they reach the desired length.

BEER STIX

4 cups all-purpose flour
1/2 cup butter or margarine
2 1/2 tablespoons sugar
3/4 to 1 cup of your favorite beer
1 eggwhite, beaten
poppyseed or sesame seed

Blend sugar with butter then add to flour in machine and mix. Add beer until dough forms pea-size lumps. Follow instructions for extruding and baking in the Cheese and Herb Sticks recipe. Before baking brush with eggwhite and sprinkle with poppy seed or sesame seed Bake at 375°F. for 8 to 10 minutes or until golden brown.

BISQUICK SNACKS

4 cups Bisquick
1 cup water
3/4 cup pepperoni, very finely chopped
1 eggwhite, beaten
poppyseed or sesame seed

Add flour and 1/2 cup of water to machine and mix. Add pepperoni and slowly add water until dough forms pea-size lumps. Using the large meat-ball die, extrude into 1-1/2" lengths and flatten slightly as you place them on a non-stick baking sheet. Brush with eggwhite and sprinkle with poppyseed. Bake at 375°F. for 8 to 10 minutes or until golden brown. Try adding finely chopped, onion, green pepper or ham instead of pepperoni.

Sauces

Chapter 3

Each recipe serves 4 to 6 people
unless otherwise indicated.

———————

Most of the recipes in this book
call for a full load of fresh pasta dough
made into a specific pasta shape using
the Automatic Pasta Maker.

———————

All of the pasta dough recipes can be
mixed and rolled by hand and many of
the shapes can be cut by hand if you
don't have a machine.

———————

You may substitute
16 ounces of dried pasta
for a full load of fresh pasta.

CURRY SAUCE

2 tart apples
medium onion, minced
2 tablespoons olive oil
2 tablespoons curry powder
1 cup light cream
1 cup coconut milk
salt and pepper to taste

Peel, core and dice the apples. Cook the apples and the onion in olive oil for 3 minutes. Add the curry powder, mix well, then add the cream, coconut milk, salt and pepper. Cook for another minute. Pureé the sauce in a blender or food processor. Return the sauce to the pan and reheat it before pouring it over the pasta.

WHITE CLAM SAUCE

2 (7-1/2 ounce) cans minced clams
2 cloves garlic, crushed
1 stick butter
3 tablespoons fresh chopped parsley

In a saucepan, sauté butter and garlic until golden brown. Drain clams, reserving all of the liquid. Stir in clam liquid and parsley; bring to a boil. Reduce heat and simmer, uncovered, for 10 minutes. Add clams and continue to simmer for about 5 minutes. A 6 ounce can tomato sauce may be added if desired.

GARLIC SAUCE

1/2 cup oil
3 or 4 anchovies, chopped (optional)
2 or 3 garlic cloves, finely minced
1/4 teaspoon black pepper
1/2 cup water

Heat oil and brown garlic until golden brown. Remove from heat; add 1/2 cup water. Season with pepper and add anchovies if desired. Simmer for 20 minutes. Toss sauce with pasta and serve immediately.

ALFREDO SAUCE

1/4 pound butter or margarine
1 cup grated fresh Romano cheese
3-1/2 cups heavy cream

Melt butter in saucepan. Add cooked, drained pasta. Add heavy cream and grated Romano cheese. Stir over low heat until desired consistency is obtained, approximately 10 minutes. Serve topped with coarse ground pepper or finely chopped fresh parsley if desired.

HOUSE PASTA

6 fresh medium tomatoes, diced
2 bunches fresh basil, shredded
1/2 cup chopped parsley
3 sun-dried tomatoes, chopped
2 tablespoons pine nuts, toasted
1/2 log Montrachet cheese, cut in small pieces
1/2 cup ripe olives, cut in half
salt and pepper, to taste
1 tablespoon Herbs de Provence
1/2 cup olive oil
1/2 cup red wine vinegar
1/4 teaspoon sugar
1/2 teaspoon Dijon-style mustard
3 garlic cloves, minced

Combine fresh tomatoes, basil, parsley, sun-dried tomatoes, pine nuts, Montrachet, olives, salt, pepper and Herbs de Provence in a large bowl and set aside. In a small bowl or blender, combine the oil, vinegar, sugar, mustard and garlic, blend well, and set aside. Cook pasta and drain. Toss the pasta with tomato and oil mixtures in a large heated bowl and serve.

SPINACH-GORGONZOLA SAUCE

4 tablespoons butter
8 ounces Gorgonzola cheese, crumbled
2 (10 ounce) packages frozen chopped spinach
1/2 cup white wine
2 large cloves garlic, finely minced
freshly ground black pepper to taste
1 to 1-1/2 cups heavy cream
Parmesan cheese

Thaw spinach, squeeze dry, and pureé. In a large saucepan, melt butter and Gorgonzola over low heat. Stir to blend, add spinach and wine. Simmer 5 to 6 minutes. Add garlic and pepper. Slowly stir in cream to form a soft, but not runny, sauce. Simmer 4 to 5 minutes. Pour sauce over pasta and serve with freshly grated Parmesan cheese.

WALNUT SAUCE

8 ounces shelled walnuts
4 tablespoons breadcrumbs
2 cloves garlic
4 tablespoons olive oil
3/4 cup milk

Blanch the walnuts in boiling water and rub off their skins. Soak the breadcrumbs in water, then drain and squeeze dry. Place the walnuts, bread-crumbs, and garlic in a blender or food processor and blend until a smooth paste forms. Add the olive oil, milk, and salt to taste and stir well. Toss cooked pasta with sauce and serve.

SPAGHETTI ROMA

3 to 4 tablespoons olive oil
1 large onion, chopped
1 celery stalk, thinly sliced
1 carrot, thinly sliced
1 cup fresh mushrooms, sliced
6 cloves garlic, minced, or more to taste
*1 pound lean ground beef **or***
1 pound Italian sausage, casings removed
1 (28-ounce) can crushed tomatoes
1 (15-ounce) can tomato sauce
1 (6-ounce) can tomato paste
2 cups water
2/3 cup red wine
2 tablespoons chopped parsley
1/4 cup fresh basil, chopped
1 teaspoon dried oregano
1 bay leaf
salt and pepper to taste
1 teaspoon sugar (optional)

Sauté onion, celery, carrot and mushrooms in the olive oil. Cook until vegetables are soft. Add the garlic and cook 1 or 2 minutes longer. Put the vegetables in a large pot. In same sauté pan, brown the meat. Add to the vegetables along with the crushed tomatoes, tomato sauce, tomato paste, water and wine. Stir to blend. Add remaining ingredients and simmer uncovered until thickened. About 1-1/2 hours. Serve over cooked pasta and pass grated fresh Romano or Parmesan cheese.

TOMATO WINE SAUCE

1 tablespoon vegetable or olive oil
1 medium-sized onion ,chopped
2 garlic cloves, minced
8 medium tomatoes, seeded and cubed
1 teaspoon sugar
1/2 teaspoon dried basil
1/3 cup red wine
3/4 cup beef broth
1 tablespoon wine vinegar
1 teaspoon salt
1 teaspoon pepper

In a large skillet, sauté the onion and garlic in oil over a medium-high heat until the onion is tender. Add the remaining ingredients to the skillet, and stir. Reduce heat, and simmer for 15 to 20 minutes, or until the mixture is heated through. Be careful not to overcook. Toss with pasta and serve.

TOMATO MEAT SAUCE

1/2 pound each lean sirloin steak
and pork tenderloin, well-trimmed
1 teaspoon olive oil
1/3 cup minced onion
1 garlic clove, crushed through a press
1 (28 ounce) can Italian tomatoes,
chopped, with their juices
1 (15 ounce) can tomato sauce
1 (6 ounce) can tomato paste
1 bayleaf
1/4 teaspoon dried oregano
1/4 teaspoon salt
1/8 teaspoon freshly ground black pepper

In a large non-stick skillet, brown the steak and pork over medium-high heat about 10 minutes. Transfer the meat to a plate and spoon fat from the skillet. Add 1/2 cup water to the skillet and bring to a boil, scraping up any browned bits from the bottom of the pan. Set the drippings aside. Heat olive oil in a large, wide non-aluminum saucepan or Dutch oven. Add the onion and sauté until tender, about 3 to 5 minutes. Add the garlic and cook 1 minute longer. Add the tomatoes with juice, tomato sauce, tomato paste, reserved drippings from the skillet, bay leaf and oregano. Add the meats and juices from the plate. Simmer on low heat, uncovered, about 1 to 1-1/2 hours, or until the meats are very tender and the sauce is reduced and flavorful. Remove meats, chop coarsely and return to the sauce. Salt and pepper to taste. Serve over your favorite pasta.

MUSHROOM-MEAT SAUCE

1 pound lean ground beef
1 pound fresh mushrooms, sliced
2 tablespoons chopped onion
1 garlic clove, pressed
1 (15-ounce) can tomato sauce
1 (10-1/2-ounce) can tomato pureé
1 cup water
2 beef bouillon cubes
1 tablespoon grated fresh Parmesan cheese
1 teaspoon dried oregano
1 teaspoon sugar
1/2 teaspoon dried basil
1/8 teaspoon black pepper
1 cup tomato juice (optional)

In a large skillet, brown meat, mushrooms, onion and garlic. Add tomato sauce, tomato pureé, water, bouillon cubes, Parmesan cheese, oregano, sugar, basil and pepper. Stir to blend ingredients. Bring to a boil, cover and reduce heat, simmering for 30 minutes. Add 1/2 to 1 cup tomato juice for a thinner sauce. Serve over your favorite fresh pasta.

44

Bolognese Tomato Sauce

2 tablespoons olive oil
1/2 cup chopped onion
1/2 cup chopped carrot
1/2 cup chopped green bell pepper
2 garlic cloves, minced
1/2 cup white wine
1 (2 pounds, 3 oz.) can peeled Italian tomatoes
1 (15 ounce) can tomato sauce
1 tablespoon chopped fresh,
or 1 teaspoon dried basil leaves,
1/2 teaspoon dried oregano
1 bay leaf
8 ounces lean ground pork
1 pound ground sirloin
1 teaspoon salt, or to taste
1/4 teaspoon coarsely ground black pepper

In a large pot, sauté onion, carrots, and green pepper in oil over low heat. Stir often, until vegetables are tender but not browned. Add garlic and sauté 2 more minutes. Pureé the whole tomatoes and add to the sauteéd vegetables. Add the tomato sauce then fill the can halfway with water and empty the water into saucepan. Add the basil, oregano, and bay leaf. Simmer, uncovered, for 15 minutes. Lightly brown pork and beef in a skillet over medium-low heat. Skim excess fat and add the meat to the tomato sauce along with drippings from the pan. Simmer sauce and meat, about 1-1/2 hours. Spoon the sauce over cooked pasta.

MARINARA SAUCE

10 cloves garlic, chopped
4 tablespoons olive oil
4 pounds fresh tomatoes OR
4 (14-1/2 ounce) cans plum tomatoes
2 teaspoons dried oregano
6 tablespoons of fresh parsley
salt and pepper to taste

Sauté garlic in olive oil. If using fresh tomatoes, remove skin by blanching in water for 30 seconds. Then cut off stem end and squeeze out seeds. If using canned tomatoes, drain the liquid. Chop tomatoes and add to pan with garlic along with remaining ingredients. Bring to a boil and simmer uncovered for about 20 minutes.

YOGURT HERB SAUCE

1/2 ounce butter or margarine
1 small onion, chopped
1 clove garlic, crushed
2 tablespoons flour
1/2 cup vegetable stock
1-3/4 cups natural yogurt
2 tablespoons fresh parsley, finely chopped
2 tablespoons fresh basil, finely chopped
2 tablespoons snipped fresh chives
freshly ground black pepper

Melt butter in a saucepan and cook onion and garlic over a medium heat for 2-3 minutes. Stir in flour and vegetable stock and cook, stirring con-

stantly, for 4 to 5 minutes longer or until sauce boils and thickens. Remove from heat, stir in yogurt and simmer over a low heat for 2 to 3 minutes longer. Mix in parsley, basil and chives and season to taste with black pepper. Spoon over pasta and serve immediately. For an interesting visual effect try using a 1/2 load each of red and green pasta dough made into spiral pasta.

WHITE WINE SAUCE

1/4 cup butter or margarine
1 small onion, finely chopped
1 bay leaf
2 parsley sprigs with long stalks
1/2 cup button mushrooms, thinly sliced
1/3 cup all-purpose flour
1-1/2 cups dry white wine
3/4 cup stock (chicken, vegetable
or fish, depending on the dish)
salt
freshly ground white or black pepper
1-1/2 cups light cream

Melt the butter in a saucepan. Add the onion, bay leaf and parsley, and cook, stirring often, for 15 minutes, or until the onion is softened slightly but not browned. Stir in the mushrooms, then stir in the flour. Gradually stir in the white wine and stock, then bring to a boil. The sauce will be too thick at this stage. Cover the pan tightly and allow the sauce to cook very gently for 15 minutes. Add the bay leaf and parsley sprigs and beat the sauce well. Remove the bay leaf and parsley sprigs. Stir in the cream and heat gently without boiling.

PESTO SAUCE

*2 cups fresh basil leaves
1 cup fresh parsley
1/2 cup each grated Parmesan & Romano Cheese
2 tablespoons pine nuts
6 blanched almonds
6 walnut halves
4 garlic cloves,
3/4 cup olive oil*

Place ingredients in a blender and blend into a smooth paste. Place mixture into a warm bowl while cooking pasta. Drain pasta and add to pesto sauce, tossing to coat. Add about 4 tablespoons of hot water and toss again. Serve immediately.

PUMPKIN CREAM SAUCE

*1 pound pumpkin cut into strips or
1 (16 oz.) can unflavored pumpkin
2-3/4 cups cream
1/2 teaspoon ground nutmeg
freshly ground black pepper
1-1/2 teaspoons snipped fresh chives*

Boil, steam, or microwave pumpkin until tender. Drain and rinse under cold running water and set aside. In a sauce pan, bring cream to a boil, then simmer about 10 minutes until reduced by half. Gently mash together pumpkin, nutmeg and pepper to taste and cook for 2 to 3 minutes longer. Add pumpkin mixture to cream, stir in chives and cook for another 2 to 3 minutes. Spoon sauce over your favorite cooked pasta and serve.

Appetizers and Side Dishes

Chapter 4

**Each recipe serves 4 to 6 people
unless otherwise indicated.**

———— ———— ———— ————

**Most of the recipes in this book
call for a full load of fresh pasta dough
made into a specific pasta shape using
the Automatic Pasta Maker.**

———— ———— ———— ————

**All of the pasta dough recipes can be
mixed and rolled by hand and many of
the shapes can be cut by hand if you
don't have a machine.**

———— ———— ———— ————

**You may substitute
16 ounces of dried pasta
for a full load of fresh pasta.**

ASPARAGUS SPAGHETTI

1 full load pasta dough made into spaghetti
2 tablespoons grated Parmesan cheese
1 pound fresh asparagus spears, trimmed
1 tablespoon olive oil
1 thick slice whole grain bread, crumbed
1 cup evaporated skim milk
2 ounces grated mozzarella cheese
freshly ground black pepper

Make and cook spaghetti in boiling water in a large saucepan. Drain, set aside and keep warm. For sauce, steam, boil or microwave asparagus until tender. Drain and refresh under cold running water. Cut asparagus into one-inch pieces and set aside. Heat oil in a frying pan and sauté bread crumbs over a low heat, stirring constantly, for 2 minutes. Add milk and asparagus, and cook, stirring occasionally, over a medium heat for 5 minutes. Mix in mozzarella and season to taste with black pepper. Put spaghetti on a warmed serving platter, spoon sauce on and toss gently to combine. Sprinkle with Parmesan cheese and serve immediately.

CHICKEN AND LEEK ROLLS

*1 full load spinach pasta made
into lasagna sheets
2 tablespoons grated fresh
Parmesan cheese
2 teaspoons vegetable oil
3 leeks, finely sliced
3 chicken breast fillets, cut into thin strips
1/2 cup chicken stock
3 teaspoons corn flour blended with
2 tablespoons water
1 teaspoon Dijon-style mustard
2 teaspoons chopped fresh basil
freshly ground black pepper*

Make and cook lasagna sheets al dente in boiling water in a large saucepan until tender. Drain, set aside and keep warm. For filling, heat oil in a large frying pan and cook leeks and chicken, stirring, for 4-5 minutes or until chicken is brown. Stir in stock, corn flour mixture, mustard and basil and cook, stirring, for 2 minutes longer. Season to taste with black pepper. Place spoonfuls of filling on lasagna sheets, roll up, top with Parmesan cheese and serve immediately.

Pasta Meatballs

1/2 teaspoon minced garlic
1/4 cup grated Parmesan cheese
1 cup tiny pasta shape, like
pastina or acine di pepe
1 pound ground turkey or veal
1 teaspoon salt
1/4 teaspoon pepper
1/4 teaspoon curry powder
1/4 teaspoon ground ginger
1 medium-sized onion, finely chopped
1 (28 to 29 ounce) jar spaghetti sauce
1/2 cup water

Preheat the oven to 325°F. In a large bowl, combine all the ingredients except the spaghetti sauce and water. Mix together, then form into 24 golf ball-sized meatballs and place on a foil-lined cookie sheet that has been coated with non-stick vegetable spray. Bake the meatballs for 8 to 10 minutes, or until brown, then immediately spoon them into a 2-quart casserole. In another large bowl, combine the spaghetti sauce and water; pour over the meatballs. Cover the casserole and bake for 30 to 40 minutes, turning the meatballs occasionally. Serve as an hors d'oeuvre, or over pasta as a main dish.

GOLDEN RAVIOLI

1 full load pasta dough made into ravioli
3/4 cup flavored bread crumbs
3/4 teaspoon garlic powder
3/4 teaspoon salt
1/4 teaspoon dried basil
1/4 teaspoon dried oregano
1/4 cup milk
1 egg, beaten
1/2 cup vegetable oil for frying
2 tablespoons grated Parmesan cheese
spaghetti sauce for dipping

Make and cook your favorite ravioli (see recipes in Stuffed Pastas chapter) to desired doneness; drain, pat dry, and cool slightly. Meanwhile, in a medium-sized bowl, combine the bread crumbs, garlic powder, salt, basil, and oregano; set aside. In another bowl, mix together the milk and egg. Dip the ravioli, a few at a time, into the milk-egg mixture, then into the bread crumb mixture to coat. In a large skillet, heat the oil. Fry the ravioli, a few at a time, until golden; drain on paper towels. Cover and chill. When ready to serve, preheat the oven to 350°F. Arrange the ravioli on a baking sheet in a single layer and sprinkle Parmesan cheese on top. Bake for 15 minutes, or until heated through. Serve hot with spaghetti sauce for dipping. Serve as an appetizer or hors d'oeuvre.

LOBSTER PASTA NETS

1 full load pasta dough made into angel hair
*3 uncooked lobster tails **or** 9 large prawns*
flour
vegetable oil for deep frying

Make and cook pasta al dente in boiling water in a large saucepan. Drain, rinse under cold running water, drain again and pat dry on absorbent paper towel. Set aside. Shell and thoroughly wash lobster or shrimp then cut into 1-1/2 inch pieces. Dust lobster pieces with flour. Wrap a few strands of pasta around each lobster piece. Continue wrapping with pasta to form a net effect around lobster. Heat oil in a large saucepan until a cube of bread dropped in browns in 50 seconds. Cook pasta wrapped lobster in batches for 2-3 minutes or until golden. Drain on absorbent kitchen paper and serve immediately with Lime Cream.

LIME CREAM

1/2 cup mayonnaise
1/4 cup sour cream
1 tablespoon finely grated lime
1 tablespoon lime juice
1 tablespoon Dijon-style mustard
*2 tablespoons chopped fresh tarragon **or***
1 teaspoon dried tarragon

Place mayonnaise, sour cream, lime rind, lime juice, mustard and tarragon in a bowl and mix to combine. Set aside.

SHRIMP EGG ROLLS

*1 full load pasta dough made into 10 egg roll
wrappers, 5 to 6 inches square
1 tablespoon vegetable oil
2 cups cooked shrimp, finely chopped
1/3 cup sliced green onion
1/2 cup chopped fresh **OR** canned bean sprouts,
1 tablespoon minced water chestnuts
1 tablespoon soy sauce
1 teaspoon grated fresh ginger root
1/4 teaspoon salt
1/8 teaspoon white pepper
1 egg slightly beaten
Oil for deep-frying
Sweet-Sour Sauce, see below*

In a wok or large skillet, heat vegetable oil over medium heat. Sauté shrimp and green onion until golden, about 2 to 3 minutes. Add bean sprouts, water chestnuts, soy sauce, ginger root, salt and white pepper. Heat 1 minute. Remove from heat. Set aside to cool. Stir beaten egg into shrimp mixture. Spread 2 tablespoons filling along 1 side of each egg roll wrapper. Fold over end of wrapper and roll up jelly-roll fashion. Dip fingers into water and moisten free edge of each egg roll. Using fingers, press edge to seal. Cover completed egg rolls with plastic wrap to prevent drying. Heat deep-frying oil to 365°F (185°C). At this temperature, a 1-inch cube of bread will turn golden brown in 50 seconds. Deep-fry egg rolls in hot oil until surface is crisp, bubbly and golden, 3 to 4 minutes. Serve with Sweet-Sour Sauce (See Recipe next page).

SWEET AND SOUR SAUCE

1/2 cup firmly packed brown sugar
1-1/2 tablespoons cornstarch
1-1/2 cups pineapple juice
1/4 cup red wine vinegar
2 tablespoons soy sauce

Combine all ingredients in a 1-quart saucepan. Cook over medium heat until sauce is thickened and clear, about 10 minutes. Set aside to cool. Makes about 2 cups.

BEEF DUMPLINGS WITH GUSTO

1 full load pasta dough
3/4 pound ground sirloin
1 medium onion, chopped
2 tablespoons olive oil
salt and pepper to taste
1 teaspoon fresh chopped marjoram
2 tablespoons fresh chopped parsley

Cook the beef and onion in the olive oil. Allow it to cool. Combine meat with remaining ingredients in a bowl and mix well. Make a load of your favorite pasta dough and use the instructions for making filled pasta at the beginning of this book. You'll need about two dozen 2 to 3 inch circles. Place a teaspoon of filling onto each round, and fold it over into a semicircle. Pinch the edges to seal them. Boil the dumplings for 10 to 15 minutes.

SESAME NOODLES

1 full load pasta dough made into vermicelli,
angel hair, or other thin pasta
1/2 cup unsalted margarine
1/2 teaspoon salt
1/2 cup sesame seeds

Make and cook the vermicelli, omitting the salt. Drain and transfer to a heated serving bowl. While the pasta is cooking, toast the sesame seeds in a small skillet over moderately low heat, stirring, until they begin to turn an amber color–about 2 minutes. Add margarine, swirling the skillet until the margarine melts. Pour the sesame seeds and margarine over the vermicelli, add the salt, and toss until each strand is coated.

ROASTED GARLIC

3 large, firm heads of garlic
1/4 cup olive oil
2 sprigs fresh thyme (optional)
salt and freshly ground black pepper to taste

Remove loose outer skin and place garlic heads in a small baking dish. Pour olive oil over garlic. Add the thyme, salt and pepper. Cover and bake at 325°F. for 1 hour. Remove from dish and let cool. Squeeze each clove to soften. This is a delicious informal appetizer served with French bread and a mild, creamy cheese. Or serve atop a half load of your favorite fresh pasta.

58

APPETIZER AND SIDE DISHES

MINI MANICOTTI QUICHES

1 full load pasta dough made into Manicotti
1/2 pound lean pork sausage or
1/2 pound sliced bacon
1/2 cup minced onion
4 eggs
1-1/2 cups half and half or
undiluted evaporated milk
1-1/2 cups shredded Swiss cheese
1 tablespoon all-purpose flour
1/4 teaspoon salt
1/4 teaspoon white pepper
1/4 teaspoon ground nutmeg
paprika

Preheat oven to 350°F. Butter 14 (2-1/2-inch) muffin cups. Make manicotti according to directions in the Making Pasta chapter. Line each muffin cup with one manicotti forming a ruffled edge. Set aside. In a large skillet, fry sausage over medium heat until cooked, stirring to break up sausage. Cool; crumble and sprinkle evenly in bottom of each Manicotti shell. Remove all fat from skillet except 1 tablespoon. Add onion to skillet. Sauté over medium heat until golden. Add beaten eggs, half and half, cheese, flour, salt, pepper and nutmeg. Spoon mixture evenly over sausage into Manicotti shells using about 2 heaping tablespoons in each shell. Sprinkle with paprika. Bake for 15 to 20 minutes. Let stand 15 minutes before serving. Serve warm or cold.
VEGETARIAN VARIATION: Substitute 1 cup cooked, chopped asparagus or broccoli for the pork

59

SMOKED FISH MOUSSE

1 half load pasta dough made into small shells
1 tablespoon butter
24 peeled and deveined shrimp
fennel leaves
*14 ounces smoked fish fillets, such as haddock **or***
salmon, skinned, cut into pieces
3 egg whites
1/2 pint whipping cream (1 cup)
salt and red (cayenne) pepper
Smelt roe (if desired)
Lime slices (if desired)

Preheat oven to 350F. Butter 6 (10-ounce) ramekins. Place 4 shrimp and a piece of fennel in bottom of each dish. In a blender or food processor, process fish until smooth. Mix in egg whites and cream. Season with salt and a pinch of red pepper. Stir in cooked pasta shells. Divide mixture among ramekins. Place dishes in a baking pan. Pour in water to come halfway up dishes. Bake about 15 minutes or until firm. Turn out onto serving plates. Garnish with roe and lime slices, if desired.

TOMATO PIE WITH STARS

*1 frozen 9-inch pie shell, thawed according
to package directions
2 teaspoons Dijon-style mustard
2 cups shredded mozzarella cheese
1/4 cup tiny pasta stars (pastina)
1 (28 ounce) can whole tomatoes, broken up,
undrained
1/2 teaspoon Italian seasoning
1/8 teaspoon pepper
1/4 teaspoon garlic powder*

Preheat the oven to 350°F. Spread the mustard on
the bottom of the thawed pie shell. Distribute 1
cup of the mozzarella cheese over the mustard,
then the pasta, tomatoes, and seasonings. Top
with the remaining 1 cup mozzarella cheese. Bake
for about 40 minutes or until golden. Allow to
stand for 10 minutes before serving. You can prepare this a few hours before mealtime, cover and
refrigerate it, then bake it just before serving.

TOMATO PASTA ROLLS

*1 full load of tomato pasta dough
made into cannelloni
1 pound frozen spinach, thawed and drained
12 ounces ricotta or cottage cheese
2 eggs
3 ounces grated Parmesan cheese
1 teaspoon ground nutmeg
freshly ground black pepper
12 slices prosciutto or thinly sliced ham
1 pound sliced mozzarella cheese*

To make filling, place spinach, ricotta cheese, eggs, Parmesan cheese, nutmeg and black pepper to taste in a bowl, and mix to combine. Make pasta according to instructions for cannelloni in the Making Pasta chapter. Cut dough into 4 x 6 inch rectangles. Spread each sheet with filling mixture, leaving a 1 inch border, then top with a slice of prosciutto or ham and mozzarella cheese. Fold in borders on long sides, then roll up from the short side. Wrap each roll in a piece of washed calico cloth and secure ends with string. Repeat with remaining ingredients. Half fill a baking dish with water and place on the stove top. Bring to a boil, add rolls, reduce heat, cover dish with aluminum foil or lid and simmer for 10 minutes. Turn rolls once or twice during cooking. Remove rolls from water and allow to cool for 5 minutes. Remove calico cloth from rolls and refrigerate until firm. To serve, cut rolls into slices. Serve on a

Soups and Stews

Chapter 5

Each recipe serves 4 to 6 people
unless otherwise indicated.

———

Most of the recipes in this book
call for a full load of fresh pasta dough
made into a specific pasta shape using
the Automatic Pasta Maker.

———

All of the pasta dough recipes can be
mixed and rolled by hand and many of
the shapes can be cut by hand if you
don't have a machine.

———

You may substitute
16 ounces of dried pasta
for a full load of fresh pasta.

EGG NOODLE VEGETABLE CHOWDER

*1 half load pasta all'uvo dough made
into fettuccini noodles and cooked al dente
1 cup diagonally sliced celery
1 medium zucchini squash, thinly sliced
1 cup fresh broccoli florets
1/2 cup thinly sliced red onion
2-1/2 cups milk
3 (10-1/2 ounce) cans condensed chicken broth
1 cup grated Cheddar cheese
1/4 teaspoon freshly ground black pepper*

In a soup kettle, combine the vegetables, milk, and chicken broth. Cover and bring to just under a boil. Reduce the heat and simmer for 15 minutes. Stir in the Cheddar cheese, salt, and pepper. Add the noodles to the vegetable mixture. Simmer for about 5 minutes or until thoroughly heated.

ONION NOODLE SOUP

*1 half load pasta dough made
into thin noodles and cooked al dente
3 tablespoons butter
3 medium onions, thinly sliced
2 tablespoons all-purpose flour
black pepper to taste
3 (10-1/2-ounce) cans beef broth
2-1/4 cups water
2 tablespoons grated Parmesan cheese*

In a 3-quart saucepan, melt butter over medium heat. Sauté onions until golden, stirring occasion-

ally. Remove onions and set aside. Stir in flour. Cook 2 to 3 minutes. Add pepper. Slowly add broth and water to the flour mixture and bring to a full boil, stirring constantly. Add noodles and sautéed onions. Cover with lid ajar and simmer 5 to 7 minutes. Remove from heat. Add Parmesan cheese. Stir until cheese melts. Serve immediately.

MINESTRONE

1 half load pasta dough made into shells
3 quarts (12 cups) beef stock
1 pound cooked beef, cubed
1 onion, peeled and chopped
1 potato, peeled and chopped
3 carrots, peeled and chopped
3 cups fresh French-cut green beans
3 cups fresh broccoli florets, chunked
1 (15 ounce) can kidney beans, undrained
chopped parsley
salt and freshly ground black pepper to taste
grated Parmesan cheese for topping (optional)

Make shells and set aside. In a soup pot, combine the beef stock, beef, onion, potatoes, and carrots. Bring to a boil, then lower the heat and simmer for 45 minutes. Add the green beans, broccoli, and kidney beans and simmer for 15 minutes more. Add pasta shells and cook until al dente. Season with parsley, salt, and pepper. Serve topped with Parmesan cheese, if desired.

66

HALF-MOON RAVIOLI & VEAL STEW

*1 full load pasta dough made into spinach and
cheese half-moon ravioli (see recipe page 144)
2 to 3 tablespoons olive oil or vegetable oil
2 pounds boneless veal shoulder
1 large onion, finely chopped
12 cloves garlic, halved
1-1/2 pounds pear-shaped (Roma-type) tomatoes,
peeled, seeded, and chopped
1 cup tomato juice
1/2 cup dry white wine
1/3 cup small ripe olives
1 or 2 small dried hot red chilies
Salt and pepper*

Cut veal into 1-1/2 inch cubes. Heat 2 tablespoons
oil in a heavy 3 to 4 quart pan over medium-high
heat. Add part of the veal and brown on all sides;
remove meat from pan as it is browned. Repeat to
brown remaining veal. Set aside. Add onion and
more oil (if needed) to pan; cook, stirring often,
until onion is soft and lightly browned (6 to 8 minutes). Stir in garlic, tomatoes, tomato juice, wine,
olives, and chilies. Return meat to pan. Bring to a
boil. Then reduce heat, cover, and simmer until
meat is tender about 1 hour. Uncover and continue
to cook, boiling gently, until sauce is thickened.
Shortly before stew is done, cook half-moon ravioli
until al dente. While ravioli are cooking, remove
chilies from stew; skim and discard fat. Season to
taste with salt and pepper. Drain ravioli well and
transfer to a warm, rimmed serving platter. Spoon
stew over ravioli and serve.

MINI MEATBALL SOUP

1 half load pasta dough made into linguini,
cut into 3/4-inch pieces
1/2 pound ground sirloin
1/4 cup dry breadcrumbs
1 egg, slightly beaten
2 tablespoons minced fresh parsley
1 tablespoon grated onion
1/2 teaspoon salt
1/8 teaspoon black pepper
1 cup water
2 (10-1/2-ounce) cans beef broth
1 beef bouillon cube
1/2 cup tomato paste
1 tablespoon butter

In a medium bowl, mix ground sirloin, bread-crumbs, egg, parsley, onion, salt and pepper. Form into about 16 meatballs by hand or by using the meatball die for your Automatic Pasta Machine. In a large saucepan, mix water, beef broth, bouillon cube, tomato paste and butter. Bring to a boil. Using a spoon, carefully lower meatballs one at a time into the broth. Cover and cook 25 minutes. Add linguini pieces and cook until pasta is al dente. Serve immediately.

PASTA E FAGIOLI

1 full load of pasta dough made into macaroni
1 cup olive or vegetable oil
6 garlic cloves, coarsely chopped
2 (14-1/2 ounce) cans diced tomatoes
1-1/2 tablespoons dried oregano
1-1/2 to 2 teaspoons pepper
1 teaspoon salt
1 teaspoon garlic powder
2 (15 ounce) cans kidney beans
3/4 cup chopped fresh parsley
1/2 cup grated Parmesan cheese

In a large saucepan, heat oil over medium-high heat; add the garlic and sauté until golden. Allow to cool slightly to prevent splattering, then add the tomatoes, oregano, pepper, salt, and garlic powder. Reduce the heat to medium and cook for 10 minutes, stirring frequently. Add the kidney beans and parsley and continue cooking for 10 minutes more, stirring frequently. Meanwhile, cook macaroni al dente; drain and add to the bean mixture. Add Parmesan cheese, mix thoroughly, and serve.

PASTA WITH LENTILS

1 half load of pasta dough made into rigatoni
1/2 cup extra-virgin olive oil
4 thin slices pancetta, coarsely chopped
1 onion, coarsely chopped
2 celery stalks, thinly sliced
1 can (14 -1/2 ounce) diced tomatoes
2 quarts water
1 cup lentils
freshly ground black pepper to taste
salt to taste
3 large handfuls chopped parsley

Heat the extra-virgin olive oil in a heavy soup pot.
Add the pancetta and onion and cook over medium
heat until the onion begins to soften. Add the celery and tomatoes. Stir well and continue to cook
for approximately 5 minutes. Add the water,
lentils, pepper, and parsley. Bring to a boil and
cook until the lentils are tender and the soup is
thick, adding water if necessary. Approximately
15 minutes before serving add rigatoni and salt to
taste. Cook at a low simmer, stirring frequently,
until pasta is tender.

Tortellini Soup

*1 half load pasta dough made into
cheese tortellini (see recipe page 144)
olive oil
2 boneless, skinless chicken breasts
3 quarts chicken broth
1 (10-ounce) package frozen chopped spinach
1/2 pound fresh mushrooms, sliced
1 medium red bell pepper, diced
1 cup cooked rice
1 tablespoon dry tarragon leaves
salt and freshly ground black pepper to taste
Parmesan cheese*

Make tortellini according to instructions for making filled pasta in the Making Pasta chapter. Cut chicken breasts into bite-sized pieces and brown in a frying pan with a little olive oil. In a large pot, bring chicken broth to a boil. Add tortellini and boil gently, uncovered, until al dente, about 6 to 8 minutes. Thaw spinach and gently squeeze out excess water. Then add spinach, chicken, mushrooms, pepper, rice and tarragon. Bring to a boil over high heat. Reduce heat immediately to simmering, cover and cook until chicken is tender. Season with salt and pepper. Garnish with a generous spoonful of Parmesan cheese.

PASTA AND POTATOES

1 full load of pasta dough made
into small macaroni
1/4 cup extra-virgin olive oil
1 onion, peeled and coarsely chopped
4 thin slices pancetta, coarsely chopped
2 stalks celery, thinly sliced
3 large carrots, peeled and cut into large pieces
1 (14 -1/2 ounce) can diced tomatoes
2 quarts water
4 potatoes, peeled and cut into 1-inch
cubes and divided
freshly ground black pepper to taste
1 sprig fresh rosemary
salt to taste

Heat olive oil in a heavy-bottomed soup pot. Add the onion and pancetta. If pancetta is unavailable, substitute lean salt pork or bacon blanched in boiling water to remove the smoked flavor. Cook over medium heat for a few minutes until the onion just begins to soften. Add the celery, carrots, and tomatoes, stir to coat with the oil, and gently sauté for 5 minutes. Add the water, half the cubed potatoes, pepper, and the rosemary. Bring the soup to a boil then simmer for about 45 minutes, stirring occasionally. The potatoes should be very soft so that the starch thickens the soup and creates a creamy texture that blends the flavors of the rosemary and tomato. Add the rest of the potatoes and salt, and cook until the potatoes are just about tender, adding more water if necessary. Then add fresh pasta and cook until al dente.

CHICKEN NOODLE SOUP

*1 half load pasta all'uvo made into linguine
and cut into 2-1/2 inch pieces
2 quarts chicken broth
2 carrots, cut into thin matchsticks
2 leeks, thinly sliced
3 cups chopped cooked chicken, diced
salt and pepper
fresh cilantro (optional)*

Bring stock to a boil in a medium-size saucepan. Add carrot and leek. Cover pan, simmer about 5 minutes or until carrot and leek are just tender to the bite. Stir in chicken, pasta, salt and pepper. Cook 5 to 10 minutes or until pasta is al dente. Garnish with cilantro, and serve at once.

ONION VERMICELLI SOUP

*1 half load of pasta dough made into vermicelli
1/2 cup butter or margarine
4 onions, thinly sliced
2 tablespoons flour
2-1/2 cups hot chicken broth
2 quarts of milk
freshly ground black pepper*

In a large pot, sauté onions in butter until soft. Gradually stir in flour then slowly add hot chicken broth. Cook, stirring constantly, until soup is smooth and thickened. Stir in milk and bring to boil. Add vermicelli and season to taste with black pepper. Continue to cook until pasta is al dente.

ORIENTAL FISH SOUP

1 half load Japanese udon, rice or
chinese egg noodle dough made
into oriental noodles
1 cup fish trimmings (bones, skins, heads)
1 quart salted water
1 pound skinned white fish fillets,
such as cod or haddock
1/2 cup dried Chinese mushrooms
3 teaspoons chopped fresh parsley
salt and freshly ground black pepper
oil for deep-frying
4 green onions, finely chopped

Soak mushrooms in water for 15 minutes, drain and remove stalks. Put fish trimmings and water into a medium-size saucepan. Bring to a boil, reduce heat, then cover and simmer for 20 minutes. In a blender or food processor, process fish until it forms a smooth paste. Add 1 teaspoon chopped parsley. Season with salt and pepper. Roll 1/2 of paste into small balls 1/2 inch in diameter. Flatten out remaining paste in a rectangular cake 2 inches wide. Cut in strips. Deep-fry strips until crisp and golden. Drain on paper towels. Keep hot. Strain fish broth through a fine sieve into a 2 quart saucepan. Bring back to a boil. Add fishballs and mushrooms. Cook gently 5 minutes. Meanwhile, cook pasta until al dente. Drain; divide among 4 heated bowls. Divide fishballs among bowls. Pour in broth. Arrange fried fish strips on top. Garnish with green onions and remaining parsley.

SPAGHETTI BEEF SOUP

*1 half load pasta dough made into spaghetti,
and cut short (3 inches)
1 pound ground sirloin
1 (16 ounce) package frozen mixed vegetables
4 cups vegetable juice cocktail or tomato juice
4 cups water
2 tablespoons instant beef bouillon
1 teaspoon dried basil leaves
1 teaspoon dried thyme leaves
1 teaspoon salt
1/2 teaspoon onion salt
1/2 teaspoon pepper
1/4 teaspoon garlic powder
2 tablespoons Worcestershire sauce
grated Parmesan cheese (optional)*

Make spaghetti and set aside. In a soup pot or
Dutch oven, brown the ground sirloin over medium-high heat. Stir in the mixed vegetables, vegetable juice cocktail, water, beef bouillon, basil,
thyme, salt, onion salt, pepper, garlic powder, and
Worcestershire sauce. Bring to a boil, reduce heat
and simmer for 30 minutes. Meanwhile, cook the
spaghetti until al dente and drain. Add the
spaghetti to the soup mixture and simmer until
pasta is thoroughly heated. Serve with Parmesan
cheese.

WEDDING SOUP

1 half load of pasta dough made into vermicelli
and cut into short lengths
8 cups beef stock (see below) **OR**
4 (14-1/2 ounce) cans chicken or beef broth
3/4 cup sweet butter, softened
1-1/2 cups freshly grated Parmesan cheese
5 egg yolks
1/4 teaspoon ground nutmeg
1-1/4 cups whipping cream
salt

In a large deep pan over high heat, bring beef stock to a boil. Add vermicelli to boiling broth. Reduce heat to medium and cook until pasta is al dente. In a bowl, combine butter, cheese, egg yolks, and nutmeg until smooth, then gradually stir in cream. Spoon a small amount of the simmering broth into cream mixture and stir to blend, then return all to the soup, stirring constantly. Immediately remove soup from heat and serve.

BEEF STOCK

3 to 4 pounds meaty beef bones
3 large onions, chopped
4 medium-size carrots, sliced
1 small turnip, chopped
2 stalks celery and their leaves, chopped
3 to 4 pounds boney chicken pieces
(necks, backs, wings)
3 pounds veal shank bones
6 sprigs fresh parsley
1/2 teaspoon black peppercorns

2 bay leaves
4 quarts water

Place meaty beef bones in a shallow baking pan large enough to hold them in a single layer. Sprinkle with 1/3 of the onion and 1/4 of the carrots. Bake, uncovered, in a 450° F oven for about 25 minutes or until meat and bones are well browned. Transfer beef bones and vegetables to 12-quart kettle. Add remaining ingredients. Bring to a boil over moderately high heat; cover, reduce heat, and simmer for 4 to 6 hours. Strain stock to remove bones and vegetables. Add salt to taste. Cover and refrigerate stock for several hours or overnight. Lift off and discard fat from surface. Leftover stock can be refrigerated for up to 5 days or frozen.

SPINACH SOUP

1 half load pasta dough made
into rotelli or fusilli cut into short lengths
8 cups chicken stock
8 ounces chopped spinach, thawed
freshly ground black pepper
4 egg yolks

Make fusilli and set aside. Place stock in a large saucepan and bring to a boil. Add pasta and spinach and cook, stirring occasionally, for 10 minutes or until pasta is al dente. Season to taste with black pepper. Place egg yolks in a small bowl and whisk to combine. Whisk a little hot soup into egg yolks, then stir egg yolk mixture into soup. Serve immediately.

WON TON SOUP

*1 full load of won ton or Chinese egg noodle dough
made into 30 won tons (see recipe page 149)
4 quarts of chicken stock **OR**
4 (14-1/2 ounce) cans chicken broth
Chinese cabbage leaves, chopped
Carrot strips
1 green onion, finely chopped*

Bring stock to a boil in a large pot. Drop won-tons, cabbage leaves and carrots into stock. Boil rapidly 2 to 3 minutes or until wontons are tender but firm. Garnish with green onion and serve.

CHICKEN STOCK

*2 (3-1/2-pound) fryer chickens with giblets
4 quarts water
2 medium-size onions
2 celery stalks
2 small bunches fresh parsley
salt and freshly ground black pepper*

Put chicken, giblets, water and onion into a large saucepan. Tie onion, celery and parsley together in a cheesecloth and add to pan with salt and pepper. Bring to a boil, reduce heat and cover. Simmer for 2 hours, occasionally removing scum from surface. Strain stock and cool, or refrigerate until following day. Remove fat from surface of stock. Makes about 4 quarts. Meat from cooked chicken can be used in other dishes. Remaining stock will keep 2 to 3 days in the refrigerator or can be frozen.

The Great *Pastamaker* Cookbook

Salads

Chapter 6

Each recipe serves 4 to 6 people
unless otherwise indicated.

———— ——— ———— ————

Most of the recipes in this book
call for a full load of fresh pasta dough
made into a specific pasta shape using
the Automatic Pasta Maker.

———— ——— ———— ————

All of the pasta dough recipes can be
mixed and rolled by hand and many of
the shapes can be cut by hand if you
don't have a machine.

———— ——— ———— ————

You may substitute
16 ounces of dried pasta
for a full load of fresh pasta.

BLACK BEAN PASTA SALAD

1 full load pasta dough made into rotini
1 tablespoon olive oil
1 (15 ounce) can black beans, rinsed and
drained (about 1-1/2 cups dried beans, cooked)
1 red bell pepper, seeded and diced
1 green bell pepper, seeded and diced
1 cup peeled jicama, diced
1/2 cup diced red onion

DRESSING
3/4 cup chopped fresh cilantro
1/2 cup defatted chicken broth
3 tablespoons orange juice
3 tablespoons red-wine vinegar
1 teaspoon ground cumin
1/2 teaspoon chili powder, or more to taste
1 tablespoon olive oil
salt
chopped chili pepper for garnish (optional)

Make rotini and cook until al dente. Drain and rinse thoroughly to cool. Place in large mixing bowl and toss with olive oil. Add beans and vegetables to pasta. For dressing, combine cilantro, chicken broth, orange juice, vinegar, cumin and chili powder in a blender. Pour into small bowl and whisk in olive oil. Pour dressing over salad and toss gently. Add salt and chili powder to taste. Garnish with chopped chili pepper and serve with

GAZPACHO PASTA SALAD

1 half load pasta dough made into
macaroni or shells
1/2 cup olive or vegetable oil
4 medium, ripe tomatoes, seeded and chopped
1/2 cup sliced green onions
1/2 cup cucumber, peeled, seeded, and chopped
1/4 cup grated Parmesan cheese
dash of hot pepper sauce
1 garlic clove, minced
2 tablespoons chopped parsley
1 tablespoon wine vinegar
1 teaspoon salt
1/2 teaspoon black pepper
Cayenne pepper to taste
1 (6 ounce) can vegetable juice

Make pasta and cook until al dente. Drain and rinse thoroughly to cool. Place in large mixing bowl and toss with olive oil. Add the remaining ingredients and combine until thoroughly mixed. Cover and chill for at least 1 hour, then mix again before serving.

CHICKEN-ARTICHOKE PASTA SALAD WITH TOMATO DRESSING

BASIL-TOMATO DRESSING
4 large ripe tomatoes, cored and finely chopped
1/4 cup chopped fresh basil
3/4 cup chopped fresh parsley
4 cloves garlic, finely chopped
4 tablespoons red-wine vinegar
2 tablespoons extra-virgin olive oil
salt and freshly ground black pepper to taste

SALAD
1 full load of pasta dough made into fusilli cut into 2-inch pieces
3 tablespoons extra-virgin olive oil
2 boneless, skinless chicken breasts
1 pound canned or frozen and defrosted artichoke hearts
salt and freshly ground black pepper to taste
sprigs of fresh basil for garnish

To make dressing combine all ingredients in a large salad bowl and set aside. Make pasta and cook until al dente. Drain and rinse thoroughly to cool. Place in large mixing bowl and toss with olive oil. While pasta cooks, place chicken in boiling water to cover. Reduce heat and poach in barely simmering water for about 15 minutes. Remove from water and cut into bite-sized cubes. Rinse artichoke hearts and cut into quarters. Add pasta, chicken and artichokes to dressing. Toss well. Taste and add salt and pepper, if needed. To serve, garnish with fresh basil sprigs.

CHICKEN PASTA SALAD

*1 half load pasta dough made into butterflies
or bowties
2 tablespoons extra-virgin olive oil
2 boneless, skinless chicken breast
3 cloves garlic
3 tablespoons white wine
1 stalk celery, diced
1 carrot, trimmed, peeled and grated
1/2 green bell pepper, seeded and diced
1 green onion, trimmed and chopped
1/2 cup mayonnaise
5 tablespoons fresh lemon juice
1 cup fresh parsley, chopped
2 tablespoons fresh dill, chopped
1 cup green or red seedless grapes, halved if large
1/3 cup chopped walnuts
salt and freshly ground black pepper to taste*

Prepare pasta according to instructions for making pasta shapes in the Making Pasta chapter. Cook until al dente. Drain and rinse thoroughly to cool. Place in large mixing bowl and toss with 1 tablespoon of olive oil. While pasta is cooking, poach chicken. Barely cover chicken with water add garlic and wine and bring to a boil. Cook chicken in barely simmering liquid about 15 minutes. Remove and let cool. Add celery, carrot, pepper and scallions to pasta. Combine mayonnaise, lemon juice, remaining 1 tablespoon oil, parsley and dill in food processor or blender and mix until smooth. Dice chicken and add to pasta. Pour dressing over and mix well. Mix in grapes and walnuts. Add salt and pepper to taste. You can make ahead and refrigerate until serving. Taste again before serving, adding more lemon juice or salt, if necessary. If desired, garnish with a few extra grapes and whole walnuts.

CONFETTI SALAD

1 half load of pasta dough made into vermicelli or oriental noodle cut into 1/4 -inch pieces
1/3 cup olive oil
3 tablespoons fresh lemon juice
1/2 teaspoon grated lemon zest
1/2 teaspoon salt
1/8 teaspoon coarsely ground black pepper
1 garlic clove, crushed
1 medium carrot, cut into 1/8-inch dice
1-1/4 cups finely diced red, green,
and/or yellow bell pepper
1/2 cup peeled, seeded, finely diced cucumber
1/4 cup finely chopped scallions
1/4 cup finely chopped red onion
1/4 cup finely chopped Italian flat-leaf parsley

Make pasta and cook until al dente. Drain (in wire mesh strainer) and rinse thoroughly to cool. Place in large mixing bowl. To make dressing, whisk oil, lemon juice, lemon zest, salt, pepper, and garlic until blended. Toss diced and chopped vegetables, pasta, and dressing together. Serve warm or at room temperature.

FRESH FRUIT SHELL SALAD

1 half load of pasta dough made into shells
1 (8 ounce) container plain low-fat or
nonfat yogurt
1/4 cup frozen concentrate orange juice, thawed
1 (20 ounce) can pineapple chunks in juice
1 large orange, peeled, sectioned, and seeded
1 cup seedless red grapes, cut into halves
1 cup seedless green grapes, cut into halves
1 apple, cored and chopped
1 banana, sliced

Make pasta and cook until al dente. Drain and rinse thoroughly to cool. Place in a bowl and set aside. To make dressing, mix the yogurt and orange juice concentrate in a small bowl. Drain juice from pineapple. In a large bowl, combine the fruit. Add the yogurt mixture and pasta; toss to coat. Cover and chill thoroughly. Toss gently before serving. This salad can be served for lunch, snack or a dessert. You can make ahead and refrigerate until ready to serve. Be sure to refrigerate leftovers.

TORTELLINI, BEEF & BROCCOLI IN RED WINE VINAIGRETTE

1 full load of pasta dough made into
cheese tortellini (see recipe page 143)
2-1/2 cups broccoli florets, chopped
1 pound deli roast beef (1/2-inch thick), cut
into 1/4 x 2-inch strips
1/2 cup red onion
1/2 cup red bell pepper
1/4 cup small black olives
2 tablespoons parsley, coarsely chopped
1/2 cup olive oil
4 tablespoons red wine vinegar
1/2 teaspoon salt
1/4 teaspoon coarsely ground black pepper
1 garlic clove, crushed

Make tortellini according to instructions for making filled pasta in the Making Pasta chapter. Cook until al dente, drain and rinse with cool water. Place in a large mixing bowl and set aside. Steam broccoli over simmering water, covered, until crisp-tender, about 3 minutes and allow to cool. Cut peppers and onions into thin slivers then add peppers, onions, broccoli, roast beef, olives and parsley in the bowl with the tortellini. To make dressing, whisk the oil, vinegar, salt, pepper and garlic until blended. Pour over salad. Let stand 30 minutes at room temperature before serving.

CHICKEN FETTUCCINI SALAD

1 half load pasta dough made into fettuccini
2 cups cubed cooked chicken
1/4 cup virgin olive oil
1/2 cup freshly grated Parmesan cheese
1/4 teaspoon garlic powder
1/4 cup chopped celery
1/4 cup chopped green bell pepper
1/4 cup sliced green onions
1/4 cup sliced mushrooms
1/2 cup small broccoli florets
1/2 cup sliced black olives
1/2 cup sliced carrots
1 cup frozen peas, thawed
1/4 cup slivered almonds

DRESSING
1/4 cup red wine vinegar
1/8 teaspoon freshly ground black pepper
1/4 teaspoon salt
1/4 teaspoon garlic powder
3/4 teaspoon dried tarragon
1/2 teaspoon dried basil
1/2 teaspoon dried oregano
1 teaspoon Worcestershire sauce
1-1/2 tablespoons Dijon mustard
juice of 1/4 lemon
1/4 cup virgin olive oil
1/4 cup water

Cook fettuccini until al dente, drain and rinse with cool water. Place in a large mixing bowl. Toss chicken and fettuccini with olive oil and allow to

cool. Add Parmesan and garlic powder and toss well. Refrigerate 1 hour or as long as overnight. To serve, add celery, green pepper, green onions, mushrooms, broccoli, olives, carrots, peas and almonds. Whisk together all dressing ingredients except water. Add water and whisk again. Pour over salad and toss thoroughly.

SMOKED SALMON PASTA SALAD

1 full load pasta dough made into bowties
or butterflies
3 tablespoons extra-virgin olive oil
12 ounces high-quality smoked salmon,
cut into thin strips
1-1/2 cucumbers, peeled, seeded and sliced
1/2 red bell pepper, seeded and diced
1-1/4 cup frozen peas
5 green onions, trimmed and chopped
1/4 cup chopped fresh dill
juice of 3 lemons
salt and freshly ground black pepper to taste

Prepare pasta according to instructions for making pasta shapes in the Making Pasta chapter. Cook until al dente. Drain and rinse thoroughly to cool. Place in large mixing bowl and toss with 1 table-spoon of olive oil. Add remaining ingredients and toss again. Add salt and pepper to taste. This salad should be served immediately, however, it will keep for several hours refrigerated. Serve at room temperature. Revive flavors, if necessary, with additional lemon juice. Garnish with more dill and/or caviar if desired.

Summer Pasta Salad

*1 full load of pasta dough made into macaroni
cut into 1/2-inch pieces
1 (16 ounce) package frozen mixed vegetables,
thawed and drained
1/4 cup finely chopped onion
2/3 cup mayonnaise
2 tablespoons lemon juice
2 teaspoons sugar
1 teaspoon dried dill weed
1 teaspoon salt
1/4 teaspoon pepper
1 cup cooked chicken or beef, diced (optional)
3/4 cup diced cheddar or jack cheese*

Make pasta and cook until al dente. Drain and rinse thoroughly to cool. Place in a large mixing bowl. Add mixed vegetables, and onion; mix well. In a small bowl, combine the mayonnaise, lemon juice, sugar, dill weed, salt, and pepper; blend well. Pour the mayonnaise mixture over the pasta-vegetable mixture and toss lightly. Add optional ingredients if desired. Chill thoroughly. Serve over lettuce and garnish with paprika. If you're not serving the salad immediately, add an additional 1/4 cup mayonnaise to moisten just before serving.

PEPPERONI, MOZZARELLA, AND BROCCOLI PASTA SALAD

*1 full load of pasta dough made into rigatoni,
rotini or shells
2/3 cup vegetable oil
1/4 cup fresh lemon juice
2 tablespoons red wine vinegar
1 teaspoon salt, or to taste
1 teaspoon dried oregano
1/4 teaspoon coarsely ground black pepper
3 cups broccoli florets, steamed until crisp-tender
(about 3 minutes)
1 whole pepperoni (about 12 ounces), skinned
and cut into 1/4-inch pieces
6 ounces mozzarella, cut into 1/4 inch pieces
1 green bell pepper, cut into 1/4-inch pieces
1/2 cup chopped red onion
1/2 cup chopped carrot (about 1 medium)
1/3 cup small brine-cured black
olives or sliced ripe black olives
1/4 cup diced (about1/4 inch) Parmesan,
Romano, or other hard sharp cheese (optional)*

Make pasta and cook until al dente. Drain and rinse thoroughly to cool. Place in a large mixing bowl and set aside. Whisk the oil, lemon juice, vinegar, salt, oregano, and black pepper together; set aside. Add broccoli, pepperoni, mozzarella, bell pepper, red onion, carrot, olives, and Parmesan, if using, to the pasta. Add dressing and toss to blend. Taste and add more salt, pepper, or lemon juice, if needed. Serve at room temperature.

WHOLE WHEAT NOODLE WITH BROCCOLI IN TAMARI DRESSING

TAMARI ALMONDS
1 tablespoon oriental sesame oil, or as needed
1 cup whole unblanched almonds
1 teaspoon fresh ginger root, grated
1 teaspoon tamari

DRESSING
3 tablespoons peanut oil
2 tablespoons tamari
1 tablespoon fresh lemon juice
1 tablespoon grated or finely shredded fresh ginger root
2 garlic cloves, crushed
2 teaspoons oriental sesame oil
1/2 teaspoon salt

SALAD
1 full load of whole wheat pasta dough made into oriental noodles cut into 8-inch pieces
3 cups fresh broccoli florets, chopped
1/2 cup green onions, thinly sliced (use white and green portion of onions)
3/4 cup cucumber, peeled, seeded and thinly sliced then cut into 1/8-inch julienne

To make tamari almonds, put just enough sesame oil in a small skillet to coat surface. Heat over very low heat; add almonds and stir to coat. Add ginger and tamari. Tamari is a soy-based sauce fermented without wheat. It is similar in flavor to soy sauce.

Sauté, stirring constantly, over low heat until almonds begin to brown slightly, about 8 minutes. Sesame oil has a very low smoking point so be careful to use very low heat.

Make pasta and cook until al dente. Drain and rinse thoroughly to cool. Place in a large mixing bowl and set aside. Steam broccoli, covered, in a steaming basket set over an inch of boiling water until crisp-tender, about 3 minutes. Rinse with cool water and set aside.

To make the dressing, whisk the peanut oil, tamari, lemon juice, ginger, garlic, sesame oil, and salt together.

To serve, toss the tamari almonds, dressing, noodles, steamed broccoli, scallions, and cucumber together. Add additional salt to taste. Try adding two cups of cooked diced chicken and serve as a main course.

TUNA MACARONI SALAD

1 full load of pasta dough made into macaroni
2 large stalks celery
1 large carrot, trimmed and peeled
1/2 onion
1 cup fresh parsley, chopped
1 (7 ounce) can water-packed tuna, drained
3/4 cup mayonnaise
1 tablespoon extra-virgin olive oil
juice of 2 lemons
2 tablespoons pickle relish (optional)
salt and freshly ground black pepper to taste

Make pasta and cook until al dente. Drain and rinse thoroughly to cool. Place in a large mixing bowl and set aside. Using food processor fitted with steel blade, finely chop vegetables and parsley separately, using pulsing action. Or chop by hand. As each vegetable is chopped, add to pasta. Add tuna. In the food processor or blender, combine mayonnaise, oil and lemon juice. Process until well mixed. Stir in pickle relish, if desired. Pour mayonnaise mixture over pasta. Mix well. Season generously with pepper and a little salt, if needed. Salad is best served immediately but can be refrigerated for several hours before serving.

94

SHRIMP NOODLE SALAD

*1 full load of rice or chinese egg noodle pasta
made into vermicelli
3/4 pound medium shrimp, peeled and de-veined
1 (1-inch) cube fresh ginger
6 tablespoons fish sauce
juice of 1 orange
juice of 1 lemon
2 teaspoons canola or peanut oil
1 red bell pepper, seeded and cut into thin strips
2 seedless grapefruits, peeled and sectioned
4 thin slices red onion, halved
1/2 cup fresh mint leaves, chopped
additional mint leaves for garnish*

Make pasta and cook until al dente. Drain and rinse thoroughly to cool. Place in a large mixing bowl and set aside. Add shrimp and ginger to medium-size pot of boiling water and poach shrimp until pink and firm, about 3 minutes. Drain, discard ginger and set shrimp aside. Combine fish sauce, orange juice and lemon juice. Whisk in oil. Pour dressing over noodles. Toss well. Add shrimp, red pepper, grapefruit, red onion and mint. Toss again. Garnish with mint leaves. Serve immediately or refrigerate for up to one day in an airtight container. Revive flavor with a little fish sauce before serving.

TUNA ANCHOVY SALAD

1 half load whole wheat pasta made into rotini
6 canned anchovies, drained
12 black olives
1 (7 ounce) can tuna, drained
1 tablespoon chopped fresh parsley
1 tablespoon fresh chives, snipped
1 hard-boiled egg, cut in wedges

MUSTARD DRESSING
1 teaspoon Dijon mustard
1 clove garlic, crushed
1 tablespoon white wine vinegar
1/4 cup olive oil
freshly ground black pepper

Make pasta and cook until al dente. Drain and rinse thoroughly to cool. Place in a large mixing bowl and set aside to cool thoroughly. Cut anchovies in half lengthwise. Wrap an anchovy strip around each olive. Place pasta, anchovy-wrapped olives, tuna, parsley and chives in a salad bowl. To make dressing ,whisk together mustard, garlic, vinegar, oil and black pepper to taste in a small bowl. Pour dressing over salad and toss to combine. Top with egg wedges. Serve on a bed of mixed greens.

SEAFOOD AND DILL SALAD

*1 half load each of pasta dough made into plain
and spinach fettuccini
1 pound firm white fish fillets, 1 inch cubes
2 tablespoons lemon juice
2 tablespoons fresh dill, finely chopped
pinch cayenne pepper
freshly ground black pepper
3 zucchini squash, cut into matchsticks
2 carrots, cut into matchsticks
2 stalks celery, cut into matchsticks*

DILL DRESSING
*1 teaspoon Dijon mustard
2 tablespoons finely chopped fresh dill
2 tablespoons lemon juice
4 tablespoons vegetable oil
freshly ground black pepper*

Place fish, lemon juice, dill, cayenne pepper and black pepper to taste in a bowl. Toss to combine and set aside to marinate for 40 minutes. Make pasta and cook until al dente. Drain and rinse thoroughly. Place in a large mixing bowl and set aside to cool thoroughly. Steam or microwave zucchini, carrots and celery separately for 2-3 minutes or until just tender. Refresh under cold running water and set aside to cool completely. Drain fish and place fish, fettuccine, zucchini, carrots and celery in a large salad bowl. To make dressing, whisk together mustard, dill, lemon juice, oil and black pepper to taste in small bowl. Pour dressing over salad and toss gently. Serve immediately.

Vegetables and Cheese

Chapter 7

**Each recipe serves 4 to 6 people
unless otherwise indicated.**

**Most of the recipes in this book
call for a full load of fresh pasta dough
made into a specific pasta shape using
the Automatic Pasta Maker.**

**All of the pasta dough recipes can be
mixed and rolled by hand and many of
the shapes can be cut by hand if you
don't have a machine.**

**You may substitute
16 ounces of dried pasta
for a full load of fresh pasta.**

CHEESE AND RED PEPPER
FETTUCCINE

1 full load of pasta dough
made into fettuccine noodles
2 tablespoons oil
2 cloves garlic, crushed
2 red peppers, cut into strips
8 green onions, cut into thin strips
1 teaspoon cracked black pepper
4 ounces feta cheese, crumbled

Make fettuccine and cook until al dente. Drain, set aside and keep warm. Heat oil in a large frying pan and cook garlic and red peppers for 2 minutes. Add green onions and black pepper and cook for 1 minute longer. Add fettuccine and cheese to red pepper mixture and toss to combine. Serve immediately. When buying feta cheese, the color of the cheese under the rind should be chalk-white. The cheese should be fresh and tangy, with no smell of ammonia.

101

TORTELLINI AVOCADO CREAM

1 full load of pasta dough made into
cheese tortellini (see recipe page 143)
1/2 ripe avocado, pitted and peeled
1/4 cup cream
1/8 cup grated fresh Parmesan cheese
1 teaspoon lemon juice
freshly ground black pepper

Make tortellini according to instructions for preparing filled pasta in the Making Pasta chapter. Cook until al dente, drain, set aside and keep warm. To make avocado cream sauce, place avocado, cream, Parmesan cheese and lemon juice in a food processor or blender and process until smooth. Season to taste with black pepper. Place tortellini in a warm serving bowl, add avocado cream and toss to combine. Serve immediately. This sauce has a tendency to discolor so make just prior to serving.

VEGETABLES AND CHEESE

VEGETABLE TAGLIATELLE

1 full load of pasta dough
made into tagliatelle
1 cup cauliflower florets, chopped
1 cup broccoli florets, chopped
4 tablespoons olive oil
2 cloves garlic, crushed
1 small eggplant, cut into strips
1/2 red pepper, cut into strips
1/2 green pepper, cut into strips
2 tablespoons chopped fresh basil
freshly ground black pepper
1/4 cup grated fresh Parmesan cheese

Make tagliatelle and set aside. Blanch cauliflower and broccoli in boiling water for 1 minute or microwave for 1 minute. Drain and refresh under cold running water, drain again and set aside. Cook tagliatelle until al dente, drain, set aside and keep warm. Heat oil in a large frying pan and cook garlic, eggplant, red pepper and green pepper over a medium heat for 4 to 5 minutes. Add tagliatelle, cauliflower, broccoli and basil to pan and toss to combine. Season to taste with black pepper and top with Parmesan cheese. Serve immediately.

SPAGHETTI WITH MUSHROOMS AND PEAS

*1 full load of pasta dough
made into spaghetti
1/2 cup olive oil
1 large clove garlic, finely sliced
6 fresh mushrooms, peeled and thinly sliced
salt
2 green onions (including green stems), sliced
2 thin slices prosciutto, diced
1 (8 ounce) can petite peas
1/2 cup dry white wine
1 tablespoon chopped fresh parsley
3 tablespoons salt
coarsely ground black pepper to taste
5 to 6 tablespoon freshly grated parmesan cheese
1 to 2 tablespoons butter (optional)*

Make spaghetti and set aside. Place half the oil and all the garlic in a small skillet and heat over a medium flame. As soon as the oil is hot, add the mushrooms and a pinch of salt. Sauté. Place the rest of the oil in another small skillet. Heat over a medium flame and add the green onions, prosciutto and salt. Sauté until the green onions are lightly browned, then add the peas. Sauté together for 5 minutes. At this point, pour the contents of both skillets into a large 10-inch skillet; mix the ingredients together well and add the wine. Let simmer for 5 minutes or until it almost comes to a boil. Sprinkle the parsley over the ingredients; turn off the flame. Cover and let stand. Cook spaghetti until al dente and drain very well. Add the pasta to the large skillet. Toss well adding black pepper and cheese. When thoroughly mixed, turn on a medium flame for 2 minutes. If it seems dry, you may add some butter while mixing. Serve hot, right from the skillet, into warmed bowls or soup platters.

Macaroni Italiano

1 full load of pasta dough made into macaroni
1/2 cup olive oil
1 yellow onion, chopped
1/2 cup chopped hearts of celery
3 bell peppers cut into 1 inch squares
2 zucchini, peeled and diced
1 medium eggplant, peeled and diced
1 teaspoon dried oregano
1/3 cup capers
1/2 cup ripe olives, sliced
4 cups marinara sauce (see recipe page 46)
1/2 cup red wine
1 tablespoon dried basil
salt and freshly milled black pepper to taste

Make macaroni and set aside. In a large skillet heat the oil; add the onion, celery, and peppers. Sauté until the peppers begin to brown. Add the zucchini, eggplant, salt, pepper, and oregano. Mix well and let simmer until tender. Add the capers, olives and marinara sauce. Mix well, cover and let simmer. Add the wine and basil, cover and let simmer for 3 more minutes. Cook macaroni until al dente and drain. Add to sauce and serve.

MACARONI AND NAVY BEANS

1 full load of pasta dough made into macaroni
1-1/2 cups dried navy beans
2 cloves minced garlic
1 onion, chopped
1/4 cup oil or 6 strips bacon, cut up
Salt and pepper to taste
2 (14 -1/2 ounce) cans diced tomatoes

Make macaroni and set aside. Cook beans slowly in 3 quarts of water until tender. Add more water as needed; set aside. Using oil or bacon, sauté onion and garlic until light brown. Add tomatoes and simmer for 10 minutes. Add to cooked beans. Meanwhile cook macaroni until al dente, drain thoroughly and add to bean and water mixture. Salt and pepper to taste. Serve immediately.

Zucchini, Mushroom, and Pimiento Lasagne

*1 full load of pasta dough made into
lasagna noodles
2 heads garlic
1 tablespoon olive oil
1 medium-size yellow onion, chopped
1 medium zucchini cut lengthwise and sliced
thin
1/2 pound mushrooms, sliced thin
1 cup fresh or frozen green peas
2 teaspoons lemon juice
1/4 teaspoon black pepper
1 (4 ounce) jar pimientos, drained and sliced
lengthwise into 1/2-inch strips
1-1/2 cups skim milk
2-1/2 tablespoons flour
1/2 teaspoon dried oregano, crumbled
1/4 cup grated Parmesan cheese*

Make lasagna sheets and set aside. Preheat the oven to 375°F. Wrap each unpeeled garlic head in aluminum foil, set in the oven, and roast for 20 minutes. Cool in the foil until easy to handle, then pull off the garlic cloves one by one and pinch, squeezing the flesh into a small bowl, mash the garlic and set aside. Cook the lasagna noodles al dente, rinse with cold water, drain and set aside to cool. Meanwhile, heat the olive oil in a heavy 10-inch skillet over moderate heat for 1 minute. Add the onion and zucchini and cook, uncovered, until soft, about 5 minutes. Add the mushrooms and cook, uncovered, 3 minutes longer. Add the peas

107

and cook 3 more minutes. Stir in the lemon juice, pepper, and pimiento and remove from the heat. In a small saucepan, whisk the milk into the flour; set over moderately low heat and cook, stirring, for 4 minutes or until thickened. Mix in the oregano, cheese, and reserved garlic. Measure out 1/2 cup of the sauce and reserve. Combine the rest with the zucchini mixture. To assemble the lasagna, line the bottom of an ungreased 8"x 8"x 2" baking pan with the cooked lasagna noodles, cutting them to fit and reserving the scraps. Spread half the zucchini mixture over the noodles, add a second layer of noodles, spread with the remaining zucchini mixture, then top with the noodle scraps. Finally, smooth the reserved sauce evenly over all. Cover with aluminum foil and bake 20 minutes; uncover and bake 15 more minutes.

BAKED SHELLS WITH MOZZARELLA

1 full load of pasta dough made into shells
3 (14 -1/2 ounce) cans diced tomatoes with juice
1 tablespoon olive oil
1 medium-size yellow onion, chopped fine
1 (8 ounce) can tomato paste
4 cloves garlic, minced
1 teaspoon dried oregano, crumbled
1 teaspoon dried basil, crumbled
1/2 teaspoon fennel seeds, crushed
1/8 teaspoon black pepper
2 cups shredded part-skim mozzarella cheese
4 tablespoons freshly grated Parmesan cheese

Make shells and set aside. Preheat the oven to 375°F. In a blender or food processor, pureé the tomatoes for 10 to 15 seconds. Set aside. Heat olive oil in a heavy 10-inch skillet over moderate heat for one minute; add the onion and cook uncovered, until soft, about 5 minutes. To crush fennel seeds and release aroma, place in a piece of plastic wrap and pound with a rolling pin or bottle. Add the tomatoes, tomato sauce, garlic, oregano, basil, fennel seeds, and pepper. Bring to a boil, reduce the heat to low, and simmer, uncovered, for 10 minutes, stirring often, until the sauce has thickened slightly. Meanwhile, cook the shells until al dente. Rinse with cold water, drain well, and place in an ungreased shallow 3-quart casserole. Cover with the sauce and sprinkle with the mozzarella and Parmesan cheeses. Bake, uncovered, for 30-35 minutes or until bubbly and golden. Let stand for 5 minutes before serving.

PENNE WITH CHICK PEAS AND TOMATOES

1 full load of pasta dough made into penne
2 tablespoons olive oil
2 cloves garlic, minced
3 (14-1/2 ounce) cans diced tomatoes with juice
1/4 teaspoon black pepper
2 tablespoons parsley, minced
1/2 teaspoon dried basil, crumbled
1/2 teaspoon oregano, crumbled
1-1/2 cups cooked and drained chick peas

Make penne and set aside. Heat the olive oil in a medium-size heavy saucepan over moderate heat for 30 seconds. Add the garlic and cook, stirring, for 30 seconds. Mix in the tomatoes, parsley, basil, oregano, and pepper; bring to a boil, lower the heat so that the mixture bubbles gently, then simmer, uncovered, for 10 minutes or until slightly thickened. Stir in the chick peas and simmer, uncovered, 10 minutes longer. Meanwhile, cook the penne until al dente, drain well and transfer to a heated serving bowl. Pour the chick pea mixture over all and toss well. Serve immediately.

Vegetables and Cheese

~~~ (decorative border) ~~~

Spaghetti with Asparagus and Pecans

1 full load of pasta dough made into spaghetti
3 tablespoons chopped pecans
1 pound asparagus, tough stems removed,
cut into 1-1/2-inch lengths
2 cloves garlic, crushed
2 tablespoons unsalted margarine
1/2 pound mushrooms, sliced thin
2 tablespoons minced fresh or freeze-dried chives
2 teaspoons lemon juice
1/4 teaspoon salt
1/4 teaspoon black pepper
1/2 cup plain low-fat yogurt

Make spaghetti and set aside. Preheat the oven to 350°F. Place the pecans on a baking sheet and toast until crisp and somewhat darker, about 7 minutes. Set aside. Meanwhile, cook the spaghetti al dente. Drain, reserving 1/4 cup of the cooking water. Rinse and set aside. At the same time, add the asparagus to a large saucepan of boiling unsalted water and cook until tender but still crisp—about 2 minutes. Set aside. Rub a heavy 12-inch skillet with the garlic, then melt the margarine in the skillet over moderately high heat. Add the mushrooms and cook, stirring frequently, for 5 minutes. Add the cooked spaghetti, asparagus, and reserved cooking water, along with the chives, lemon juice, salt, and pepper. Toss well with two serving forks. Add the yogurt and pecans and cook, tossing, until heated through, about 2 to 3 minutes longer. Serve immediately.

Pasta, Cheese, and Tomato Pie

1 full load of pasta dough made into linguine
2 tablespoons olive oil
1 medium-size yellow onion, chopped fine
3 cloves garlic, minced
1/4 cup parsley, minced
2 tablespoons lemon juice
1-1/2 teaspoons dried oregano, crumbled
2 teaspoons dried basil, crumbled
1/4 teaspoon white or black pepper
3/4 cup part-skim ricotta cheese
2 large egg whites
1/4 cup freshly grated Parmesan cheese
3 medium-size ripe tomatoes, sliced thin
1/2 cup shredded part-skim mozzarella cheese

Make linguine and set aside. Preheat the oven to 375°F. Lightly grease and flour an 10-inch spring-form pan and set aside. Cook the linguine al dente. Drain, rinse under cold running water, and drain again. Return to the cooking pot and set aside. Meanwhile, heat the olive oil in a heavy 7-inch skillet over moderate heat for 1 minute. Add the onion and garlic and cook, uncovered, until the onion is soft, about 5 minutes. Add to the linguine along with the parsley, lemon juice, 1 teaspoon of the oregano, 1/2 teaspoon of the basil, and the pepper. Toss well. In a small bowl, combine the ricotta cheese, egg whites, 2 tablespoons of the Parmesan cheese, and the remaining oregano and basil. Add to the linguine and toss well. Turn half the linguine-cheese mixture into the prepared pan and press lightly over the bottom. Arrange half the tomato slices on top and sprinkle with half the mozzarella cheese. Repeat the layers, using the remaining linguine, tomatoes, and mozzarella. Sprinkle the remaining Parmesan cheese on top. Cover with aluminum foil and bake for 40 minutes or until set. Remove the foil and bake 5 minutes longer. Cool for 10 minutes, then gently loosen the pie around the edges with a thin-bladed knife, remove the springform pan sides, and cut pie into wedges.

MANICOTTI WITH RICOTTA AND PEAS

1 full load of pasta dough made into manicotti
1/2 cup fresh or frozen green peas
1-1/2 cup part-skim ricotta cheese
3 tablespoons golden raisins
2 large eggs
1 large egg white
4 medium ripe tomatoes, chopped
3 tablespoons minced fresh mint or parsley
1/2 teaspoon black pepper
2 tablespoons tomato paste

Preheat the oven to 375°F. Make manicotti and cook al dente, drain, rinse and set aside. Bring an inch of water to a boil in a small saucepan, add peas and cook for two minutes. Drain. In a medium bowl, combine the peas, cheese, raisins, eggs, egg white, 1/2 cup tomatoes, 1-1/2 tablespoons of mint, and 1/4 teaspoon pepper and mix well.

Stuff manicotti shells with the mixture. Combine the remaining tomatoes, mint, and pepper with the tomato paste in a small bowl and mix well. Pour 3/4 cup of the mixture into the bottom of an ungreased 8" x 8" x 2" baking pan and place the filled pasta shells on top. Pour the remaining mixture over all. Cover with aluminum foil and bake for 20 minutes. Uncover and bake 10 minutes longer.

Light

Pastas

Chapter 8

Each recipe serves 4 to 6 people
unless otherwise indicated.

———————

Most of the recipes in this book
call for a full load of fresh pasta dough
made into a specific pasta shape using
the Automatic Pasta Maker.

———————

All of the pasta dough recipes can be
mixed and rolled by hand and many of
the shapes can be cut by hand if you
don't have a machine.

———————

You may substitute
16 ounces of dried pasta
for a full load of fresh pasta.

ALFREDO-STYLE NOODLES

1 full load of pasta dough made into fettuccini
1/2 cup part-skim ricotta cheese
1/4 cup plain low-fat yogurt
1/2 cup grated Parmesan cheese
2 tablespoons unsalted margarine
1/4 teaspoon black pepper

Make fettuccini and cook al dente. Drain well and return to the cooking pot. Add the ricotta cheese, yogurt, Parmesan cheese, margarine, and pepper, and toss well to mix. Transfer to a warm platter and serve with a cooked green vegetable

VARIATIONS
Noodles with Mushrooms–Melt the margarine in a heavy 10-inch skillet over moderate heat. Add 1-1/2 cups sliced mushrooms and cook, stirring, for 3 to 5 minutes. Toss with the noodles and the remaining ingredients.

Noodles with Onion and Garlic–Melt the margarine in a heavy 7-inch skillet over moderate heat. Add 1 large yellow onion, sliced, and 1 clove garlic, minced. Cook, uncovered, until the onion is soft—about 5 minutes. Toss with the noodles and the remaining ingredients.

FUSILLI WITH PARSLEY-MUSHROOM SAUCE

1 full load of pasta dough made into fusilli
1 cup plain low-fat yogurt
1/2 cup grated Parmesan cheese
1/2 cup minced parsley
4 tablespoons sour cream
1/4 teaspoon black pepper
2 tablespoons olive oil
1 cup mushrooms, sliced thin
1 medium-size yellow onion, chopped
3 cloves garlic, minced
1/2 cup dry white wine
parsley sprigs (optional)

Make fusilli and set aside. In a small bowl, combine the yogurt, cheese, parsley, sour cream, and pepper; cover and refrigerate. Meanwhile, heat the olive oil in a heavy 7-inch skillet over moderately high heat for 1 minute. Add the mushrooms, onion, and garlic and cook, stirring occasionally, for 5 to 7 minutes or until the onion is soft. Add the wine to the mushroom mixture and cook for 1 to 2 minutes or until most of the liquid is absorbed. Add the yogurt-cheese mixture and heat through; do not boil or the sauce will curdle. Cook fusilli al dente, drain well and return to the cooking pot. Add the mushroom mixture to the pot and toss well with two forks to mix. Transfer the pasta to a heated platter and garnish with parsley sprigs, if desired.

118

PAPPARDELLE WITH SPINACH SAUCE

1 full load of pasta dough made into pappardelle
2 tablespoons olive oil
1 large yellow onion, chopped fine
4 cloves garlic, minced
2 pounds fresh spinach, chopped, OR
2 (10 ounce) packages frozen spinach,
thawed and well drained
1 cup skim milk
1 cup low-sodium chicken broth
1/2 cup grated Parmesan cheese
1/2 teaspoon black pepper

Make pappardelle and set aside. Heat the olive oil in a small heavy sauce pan over moderate heat for 1 minute; add the onion and garlic and cook, uncovered, until the onion is soft—about 5 minutes. Add the spinach, milk, chicken broth, cheese, and pepper. Bring the mixture to a boil; reduce the heat and simmer, uncovered, for 3 minutes or until the sauce thickens slightly. Pour the sauce into an electric blender or food processor and whirl until the mixture is puréed. Pour the sauce back into the saucepan and reheat over moderate heat until the mixture starts to simmer—about 1 minute. Cook pappardelle al dente, drain well and return to the cooking pot. Add the spinach mixture to pasta and toss well with two forks to mix. Transfer to a heated platter and serve. VARIATION: Substitute 3 cups chopped broccoli florets for spinach and pureé as directed.

119

LINGUINE WITH WHITE CLAM SAUCE

1 full load of pasta dough made into linguine
3 tablespoons olive oil
1 small yellow onion, chopped fine
10 cloves garlic, minced
4 tablespoons flour
1/2 cup dry white wine
1/2 cup clam juice or low-sodium chicken broth
2 cups low-sodium chicken broth
2 (6-1/2 ounce) cans minced clams, drained
rinsed well, and drained again
1/2 cup grated Parmesan cheese
4 tablespoons minced parsley

Make linguine and cook al dente. Rinse with cold water, drain, and set aside. Meanwhile, heat the olive oil in a heavy 10-inch skillet over moderate heat for 1 minute. Add the onion and garlic and cook, uncovered, until the onion is soft—about 5 minutes. Blend in the flour and cook, stirring constantly, for 1 minute. Add the wine and cook for 2 minutes, stirring constantly. Add the clam juice and chicken broth and cook, stirring, 4 minutes longer. Stir in the clams and cheese. Add the linguine and cook 1 minute longer, tossing well until heated through. Mix in the parsley and serve with a tossed green salad and crusty bread.

VARIATION: Linguine with Red Clam Sauce - Omit the flour. Add 1 cup drained and chopped canned low-sodium tomatoes along with the clam juice and chicken broth. Cook and stir for 6 minutes or until slightly thickened, then proceed with the recipe as directed.

FISHERMAN'S BAKED SHELLS

1 full load of pasta dough made into shells
2 tablespoons olive oil
2 large yellow onions, chopped
2 clove garlic, minced
2 medium-size carrots, peeled and chopped fine
2 medium-size stalks celery,chopped fine
2 small red peppers, seeded, and chopped fine
1 teaspoon each dried basil, marjoram,
and rosemary, crumbled
1/2 teaspoon black pepper
1 cup dry white wine
4 tablespoons flour
3-1/2 cups low-sodium chicken broth
2 (6-1/2 ounce) cans water-packed light tuna,
drained and flaked
1/4 cup grated Parmesan cheese
2 tablespoon lemon juice
1/2 cup minced parsley

Make shells and set aside. Heat the olive oil in a heavy 12-inch skillet over moderate heat for 1 minute. Add onion, garlic, carrot, celery, red pepper, basil, marjoram, rosemary, and black pepper. Cook, uncovered, stirring occasionally, until the vegetables are soft, about 5 to 8 minutes. Add the wine to the skillet and boil, uncovered, for 3 minutes. Place the flour in a small bowl and add enough of the chicken broth, a tablespoon at a time, to make a smooth paste. Blend in the rest of the chicken broth and add the mixture to the skillet. Cook, stirring constantly, until slightly thickened, about 3 minutes. Lower the heat so that the

The Great *Pastamaker* Cookbook

mixture bubbles gently, cover, and simmer for 8 minutes or until the sauce has thickened. Meanwhile, preheat the oven to 350°F. Cook the shells, drain well and place in an ungreased 3-1/2-quart casserole. Add the tuna but do not mix. Stir the cheese, lemon juice, and half the parsley into the sauce. Pour over the tuna and pasta shells and toss well to mix. Cover and bake for 20 minutes. Sprinkle with the remaining parsley and serve.
Tip: Water-packed tuna not only tastes better than tuna packed in oil, but also has less than a gram of fat per can. Oil-packed tuna has as many as 20 grams of fat per can and almost twice the calories.

TORTELLINI IN BROTH

*1 full load of pasta dough made into cheese, spinach or meat tortellini
(see recipe in stuffed and specialty chapter)
2 quarts reduced-sodium chicken broth
2 tablespoons grated Parmesan cheese
3 cups spinach, arugula or watercress leaves*

Make tortellini according to instructions for making stuffed pasta in the Making Pasta chapter. Cook tortellini until al dente and drain thoroughly. Meanwhile, heat the chicken broth in a medium saucepan. Add greens and cook until tender. Add drained tortellini to the broth. Bring to a gentle boil. Ladle into soup bowls and sprinkle grated Parmesan cheese over each serving.

SPAGHETTI WITH MEAT AND TOMATO SAUCE

1 full load of pasta dough made into spaghetti
1 tablespoon olive oil
1 medium-size yellow onion, chopped fine
1 medium-size carrot, peeled and chopped fine
1 small stalk celery, chopped fine
2 cloves garlic, minced
1/2 pound very lean ground sirloin
3 (16 ounce) cans low-sodium tomatoes,chopped,
with their juice
2 tablespoons minced fresh basil or
1 teaspoon dried basil, crumbled
1/4 teaspoon black pepper

Make spaghetti and set aside. In a large saucepan, heat olive oil for 1 minute over moderate heat. Add onion, carrot, celery, and garlic, and cook, stirring frequently, until the onion is soft, about minutes. Add ground sirloin and cook, stirring, until browned, about 3 to 5 minutes. Add tomatoes, basil, and pepper, reduce heat to low, and simmer, uncovered, stirring occasionally, for 1 hour or until thickened. When sauce has only about 10 minutes longer to simmer, cook the spaghetti, drain well and place in a large heated serving bowl. Add the sauce and toss well. Serve immediately.

PASTA WITH BROCCOLI IN SWEET TOMATO SAUCE

1 full load of pasta dough made into fettuccine
5 cups broccoli florets (1 medium-size head)
2 tablespoons olive oil
3 cloves garlic, minced
5 large ripe tomatoes (about 2 pounds), peeled, cored, and chopped, OR 1 large (28 ounce) can low-sodium tomatoes, chopped, with their juice
3 tablespoons golden raisins, chopped
1/8 teaspoon cayenne pepper
2 tablespoons whole pine nuts
or chopped almonds
3 tablespoons minced parsley

Make fettuccine and set aside. In a large saucepan, cook the broccoli in enough boiling unsalted water to cover until just tender, about 2 to 3 minutes. Rinse under cold running water, drain, and set aside. In another large saucepan, heat the olive oil over moderately low heat for 30 seconds; add the garlic and cook, uncovered, until golden, about 3 minutes. Add the tomatoes, raisins, and cayenne pepper, and simmer, uncovered, for 15 minutes. Add the pine nuts and simmer 5 minutes longer. Meanwhile, cook the spaghetti, drain well and place in a large heated serving bowl. Add the cooked broccoli to the warm tomato sauce, tossing to heat through. Pour over the pasta and sprinkle with the parsley.

CRAB AND PASTA SALAD

1 half load of pasta dough made into vermicelli
2 tablespoons Oriental sesame or peanut oil
1 red or green pepper, cored, seeded, and cut into
matchstick strips
2 cloves garlic, minced
3 green onions, sliced thin
10 ounces fresh, thawed frozen, or canned
crabmeat, washed thoroughly
1 head romaine lettuce torn into bite-size pieces
2 tablespoons reduced-sodium soy sauce
2 tablespoons red wine vinegar
1 tablespoon medium-dry sherry or white wine
1/2 teaspoon sugar
1/8 teaspoon cayenne pepper

Make vermicelli and cook until al dente. Drain and transfer to a serving bowl to cool. Meanwhile, heat 1 tablespoon of the sesame oil in a heavy 10-inch skillet over moderately high heat for 1 minute; add the red pepper and garlic and stir-fry just until limp, about 3 minutes. Add the green onions and stir-fry 30 seconds longer. Combine the vermicelli, red pepper-green onion mixture, crabmeat, and lettuce in a large bowl. In a small bowl, whisk together the remaining sesame oil and the soy sauce, vinegar, sherry, sugar, and cayenne pepper. Pour over the pasta mixture, tossing gently to mix.

BOWTIES WITH KASHA AND ONIONS

1 full load of pasta dough made into bowties
3 tablespoons olive oil
2 yellow onions, sliced thin
1/2 pound mushrooms, sliced thin
1 cup kasha (toasted buckwheat)
2 large eggs, slightly beaten
1/4 teaspoon salt
1/4 teaspoon black pepper
3 cups hot water

Make bowties and set aside. Heat the olive oil in a heavy 12-inch skillet over moderate heat for 1 minute. Add the onions and cook, stirring frequently, until they start to brown—about 10 minutes. Meanwhile, cook the bowties al dente. Rinse with cold water, drain well, and set aside. Add the mushrooms to the skillet and cook, stirring occasionally, for 5 minutes or until the mushrooms are lightly browned and their juices have evaporated. In a small bowl, combine the kasha and egg, stirring well to coat each grain. Push the mushroom-onion mixture to one side of the skillet, add the kasha-egg mixture to the other, raise the heat to high, and stir the kasha until the grains have separated, about 4 minutes. Add the salt, pepper, and hot water and stir to mix the contents of the skillet. Cover, reduce the heat to moderately low, and cook, stirring occasionally, for 15 minutes or until the kasha is tender. Stir in the cooked bowties and bring to serving temperature.

ROTINI WITH EGGPLANT AND BEEF

1 full load of pasta dough made into rotini
1/2 pound ground sirloin
2 tablespoons olive oil
1/2 cup chopped onion
2/3 cup red bell pepper, diced (1/4 inch)
1 eggplant, peeled and cut into 1/2-inch cubes
1/2 cup beef broth, preferably unsalted
1-1/2 cups tomato, coarsely chopped
1 garlic clove, crushed through a press
1/4 teaspoon salt
salt and freshly ground black pepper to taste
2 tablespoons grated Parmesan cheese

Make rotini and set aside. Cook the ground sirloin in a large skillet over medium-high heat, until browned, about 10 minutes. Transfer to a strainer to drain off the fat. Wipe out the skillet, add the olive oil and heat over medium heat. Add the onion and bell pepper; stir to coat with the oil. Add the eggplant, raise the heat to high and cook, stirring often, 5 minutes. Add the beef broth and cook, stirring often, until the broth is absorbed, about 5 minutes. Add the beef, chopped tomato and garlic. Cover, reduce the heat, and cook until the eggplant is tender, about 10 minutes. Uncover and cook until some of the liquid is evaporated and the sauce is slightly thickened, about 3 minutes. Season with the salt and pepper. Meanwhile, cook the rotini until al dente and drain well. Transfer the pasta to a large serving bowl. Top with the sauce and toss. Sprinkle the Parmesan cheese over the top and serve.

VEGETABLE LASAGNE

1 full load of pasta dough made into lasagna
2 teaspoons olive oil
1 cup fresh mushrooms, thinly sliced
1/2 cup onion, finely chopped
1/2 cup finely chopped peeled carrot
1 garlic clove, crushed through a press
2 cups chopped fresh spinach (tightly packed)
1/8 teaspoon salt
1/8 teaspoon freshly ground black pepper
1 cup reduced-fat or part-skim ricotta cheese
2 tablespoons parsley or fresh basil, chopped
2 tablespoons grated Parmesan cheese
1 recipe light marinara sauce (recipe follows)
1-1/2 cups part-skim mozzarella cheese,
coarsely shredded

Make lasagna to fit your baking dish, cook until al dente, rinse and set aside. Heat the olive oil in a large non-stick skillet. Add the mushrooms, onion and carrot and cook over medium heat, stirring, until the carrot is tender, 8 to 10 minutes. Raise the heat to high and cook, stirring, until any excess moisture is evaporated. Add the garlic and cook 1 minute. Stir in the spinach until blended. Cover and cook over low heat until the spinach is wilted, about 3 minutes. Season with the salt and pepper. Remove from the heat. In a food processor, combine the ricotta cheese, parsley and 1 tablespoon of the Parmesan cheese. Purée until smooth and creamy. Set the flavored ricotta aside. Preheat the oven to 350° F. Select a shallow baking dish about 9 X 13 inches. Spread 1/2 cup of the marinara sauce in the bottom of the dish. Cover the bottom with lasagna. Evenly spoon the spinach mixture over the pasta. Sprinkle 1/4 cup of the mozzarella cheese over the filling. Top with more of the lasagna noodles. Spread the flavored ricotta over the noodles and sprinkle another 1/4 cup mozzarella cheese over the ricotta. Top with remaining lasagna noodles, marinara sauce and cheese. Cover the dish with aluminum foil and bake 30 minutes. Uncover and bake 20 minutes, or until the top is bubbly and browned. Let stand 10 minutes before serving.

LIGHT MARINARA SAUCE

1 tablespoon olive oil
1/4 cup finely chopped onion
1 small garlic clove, crushed
1 (28 ounce) can Italian-style plum tomatoes,
with their juices, pureed if desired
2 tablespoons parsley or fresh basil, chopped
1 teaspoon minced fresh oregano or thyme
1/4 teaspoon salt
1/8 teaspoon freshly ground black pepper

Heat olive oil in a large skillet. Add the onion and cook over medium-low heat, stirring, until tender, 3 to 5 minutes. Do not brown. Add the garlic and cook 1 minute longer. Add tomatoes with their juices. Bring to a boil, breaking up the tomatoes if they have not been puréed. Simmer over medium heat, stirring occasionally until slightly thickened, about 25 minutes. Stir in the parsley, oregano, salt and pepper. Makes about 2 cups.

PASTA AND BEAN SOUP

1 half load of pasta dough made into shells
1 cup (about 1/2 pound) dried cannelloni, or
other white bean, rinsed with grit removed
1 tablespoon olive oil
1 thin slice of prosciutto, pancetta or smoked
ham, finely diced (about 1 tablespoon)
1/2 cup chopped onion
1/2 cup sliced celery
1/2 cup carrot, diced (1/4 inch)
2 garlic cloves, minced
1 (14 ounce) can plum tomatoes, with juices
1 bay leaf
1/2 teaspoon salt
3 tablespoons grated Parmesan cheese

Make shells and set aside. In a large saucepan or
Dutch oven, cover beans with water and soak
overnight. Or combine the beans and water in a
large pot, bring to a boil and cook, uncovered, 1
minute. Then remove pan from the heat, cover
and let stand 1 hour. Drain well. Heat olive oil in
a Dutch oven. Add the prosciutto, onion, celery
and carrot and cook over low heat, stirring occasionally, until tender. Add the garlic and cook 1
minute longer. Add the drained beans, 8 cups of
water, tomatoes and bay leaf. Bring to a boil,
reduce the heat to low and cook, uncovered, until
the beans are very tender and the soup is thickened, about 2 hours. Stir in the pasta and salt.
Simmer, stirring often, until the pasta is al dente.
Stir in 1-1/2 tablespoons of the Parmesan cheese.
Serve in bowls and top with remaining Parmesan.

LINGUINE WITH PANCETTA AND ARUGULA

1 full load of pasta dough made into linguine
1 tablespoon olive oil
1/2 cup slivered red bell pepper
2 thin slices of pancetta, prosciutto, or Black
Forest Ham, minced (about 2 tablespoons)
3 cloves garlic, thinly sliced
1 bunch of arugula, stemmed, trimmed and
drained (about 2 cups slightly packed)
or watercress can be substituted

Make linguine and set aside. In a large skillet, preferably non-stick, combine the olive oil, red pepper, pancetta and garlic. Cook over medium-low heat until the garlic is golden and the pepper is tender, about 5 minutes. Remove from the heat, cover and keep warm. Meanwhile, cook the linguine until al dente. Ladle about 1/4 cup of the pasta cooking liquid into a large serving bowl. Drain the pasta. Stir the arugula into the pasta cooking liquid in the serving bowl just until wilted. Add the cooked pasta and toss to blend. Drizzle the red pepper and oil mixture over the pasta, toss gently and serve.

PENNE WITH ARUGULA AND RED ONION

1 full load of pasta dough made into penne
2 small bunches of arugula
2 tablespoons extra virgin olive oil
2/3 cup thinly sliced red onion
1 garlic clove, crushed
2 tablespoons grated Parmesan cheese

Make penne and set aside. Trim any roots and thick stems from the arugula. Wash the arugula in several changes of cold water and drain well. There should be about 3 cups packed. Heat the olive oil in a large skillet. Add the red onion and cook, stirring, until tender, about 5 minutes; do not brown. Add the garlic and cook 1 minute. Stir in the arugula leaves and cook, stirring, until wilted and coated with the oil, about 2 minutes. Meanwhile, cook penne until al dente and drain reserving about 1/2 cup of the pasta cooking liquid in a large serving bowl. Add drained pasta to the serving bowl. Add the arugula mixture and toss. Sprinkle with the Parmesan cheese and serve.

PASTA SHELLS WITH WINTER VEGETABLES

1 full load of pasta dough made into shells
12 garlic cloves, peeled
3/4 cup reduced-sodium chicken broth
2 tablespoons olive oil
1 cup thinly sliced peeled carrots
1 cup diced peeled sweet potato OR
butternut squash
1 cup diced unpeeled red potatoes
1 cup broccoli florets
1 cup cauliflower florets

Make shells and set aside. In a small saucepan, combine the garlic and chicken broth. Bring to a boil, reduce the heat to low, cover and cook until the garlic is very soft, about 20 minutes. Remove from the heat, uncover and let cool slightly. Transfer the garlic and broth to a food processor and purée until smooth. Add the olive oil and purée until blended. Boil the shells for 3 minutes, but do not drain. Add the carrots, sweet potato and red potatoes to the pasta and boil 5 minutes. Add the broccoli florets and cauliflower florets and boil 3 to 5 minutes longer, or until the pasta is al dente and the vegetables are tender. Ladle 1/2 cup of the pasta cooking liquid into a large serving bowl. Drain the pasta and vegetables. Add the pasta and vegetables to the serving bowl. Scrape the garlic purée over the pasta and toss to mix. Serve at once.

LINGUINE WITH ZUCCHINI AND CARROT SAUCE

1 full load of pasta dough made into linguine
or fettuccine
1/4 cup olive oil
1 cup sliced red onion
1-1/2 cups coarsely shredded peeled carrot
1-1/2 cups reduced-sodium chicken broth
1-1/2 cups coarsely shredded zucchini
2 cloves garlic, crushed through a press
salt and freshly ground black pepper to taste

Make linguine and set aside. Cut onion, carrots, and zucchini into strips to match the width of the pasta. Heat the olive oil in a medium skillet then add the onion and cook over low heat, stirring, until crisp-tender, about 2 minutes. Meanwhile cook pasta until al dente, drain and transfer to a heated serving platter. Add the carrot and chicken broth to the onions and bring to a boil. Simmer over medium-low heat for 2 minutes. Add the zucchini and garlic and cook, stirring often, until the zucchini is barely tender, 1 to 2 minutes. Season with the salt and a generous grinding of pepper. Pour over pasta, toss, and serve immediately.

Stuffed and Specialty

Chapter 9

Each recipe serves 4 to 6 people
unless otherwise indicated.

———— ———— ———— ————

Most of the recipes in this book
call for a full load of fresh pasta dough
made into a specific pasta shape using
the Automatic Pasta Maker.

———— ———— ———— ————

All of the pasta dough recipes can be
mixed and rolled by hand and many of
the shapes can be cut by hand if you
don't have a machine.

———— ———— ———— ————

You may substitute
16 ounces of dried pasta
for a full load of fresh pasta.

THREE-CHEESE CANNELLONI

1 full load of pasta dough made into cannelloni
8 ounces ricotta cheese
1 cup freshly grated Parmesan cheese
2-1/2 cups fresh white bread crumbs
1 teaspoon dried oregano
1 bunch watercress, trimmed and chopped
salt and freshly ground black pepper to taste
freshly grated nutmeg
2 cups of marinara sauce (see recipe page 46)
8 ounces mozzarella cheese, thinly sliced
handful of fresh basil sprigs

Make cannelloni according to instructions for cutting pasta shapes in the Making Pasta chapter. You'll need about 18 squares, 4 x 4-inch. Cook the pieces of pasta, a few at a time if necessary, until al dente. Drain and rinse under cold water, then lay out on paper towels. Preheat the oven to 400°F. Mix the ricotta, Parmesan, bread crumbs, oregano and watercress. Add seasoning and a little grated nutmeg to taste, then stir the mixture to make sure all the ingredients are thoroughly combined. Butter a shallow ovenproof dish. Place some of the cheese mixture on a piece of pasta, then roll it up into a neat tube and place in the dish with the seam side down. Repeat with the remaining pasta and filling. Ladle the tomato sauce over the cannelloni, then top with the mozzarella. Bake for 25-30 minutes, until the cheese has melted and browned. Use scissors to shred the basil leaves and soft stems and sprinkle over the cannelloni. Serve at once.

SARDINE & MUSHROOM CANNELLONI

1 full load of pasta dough made into cannelloni
2 (4 ounce) cans sardines in oil
1 onion, chopped
2 garlic cloves, crushed
1-3/4 cups fresh white bread crumbs
2/3 cup mushrooms, chopped
2/3 cup low-fat soft cheese
1 cup grated Cheddar cheese
2 cups of marinara sauce (see recipe page 46)
grated peel and juice of 1 lemon
salt and freshly ground black pepper

Make cannelloni according to instructions for cutting pasta shapes in the Making Pasta chapter. You'll need about 18 squares, 4 x 4-inch. Cook the pieces of pasta, a few at a time if necessary, until al dente. Drain and rinse under cold water, then lay out on double-thick paper towels. Preheat the oven to 400°F. Pour the oil from the sardines into a small saucepan. Add the onion and garlic, then cook, stirring often, for 10 minutes. Remove from the heat. Mash the sardines and add them to the onion and garlic. Mix in the bread crumbs, mushrooms, soft cheese, three-quarters of the Cheddar cheese, the lemon peel and juice, and seasoning to taste. Butter a shallow ovenproof dish. Place some of the sardine mixture on a piece of pasta, then roll it up into a neat tube and place in the dish with the seam side down. Repeat with the remaining pasta and filling. Ladle the marinara sauce over the cannelloni, then sprinkle with the remaining cheese. Bake for 25-30 minutes, until the cheese has melted and browned. Serve at once. The sardine and cheese mixture also makes a good filling for ravioli, tortellini or cappelletti.

PORK AND ROSEMARY RAVIOLI

1 full load of pasta dough made into ravioli
2 tablespoons olive oil
1 onion, finely chopped
2 garlic cloves, crushed
4 juniper berries, crushed
1 tablespoon chopped rosemary
1/2 teaspoon ground mace
14 ounces lean ground pork
1 cup fresh white bread crumbs
1/2 cup chopped mushrooms
salt and freshly ground black pepper
2 eggs
2 tablespoons fresh parsley, chopped
freshly grated Parmesan cheese

Heat the oil in a saucepan. Add the onion, garlic and juniper berries. Cook, stirring for 15 minutes, or until the onion is softened. Stir in the rosemary, mace, pork, bread crumbs, mushrooms and salt and pepper to taste. Add 1 egg and thoroughly mix the ingredients, mashing them with the back of the spoon. Make ravioli according to instructions for making filled pasta in the Making Pasta chapter. You can assemble ravioli as directed using the Ravioli Cutter for smaller shapes to make about 80 ravioli or by hand method to make larger shapes. Beat the remaining egg. Be sure to brush bottom layer of dough with egg before placing stuffing on it and then covering with the top layer of dough. Pinch the edges of the dough together to seal. Cook the ravioli until al dente. Do this in batches if necessary, then drain the pasta. Make white wine sauce (see below) but do not add the cream or mushrooms until just before you have completed cooking the ravioli. Pour the sauce over the ravioli and garnish with parsley and Parmesan cheese.

WHITE WINE SAUCE

1/4 cup butter or margarine
1 onion, finely chopped
1 bay leaf
3 parsley sprigs with stems
1 cup mushrooms, thinly sliced
1/3 cup flour
1-1/4 cups dry white wine
1 cup chicken broth
salt and freshly ground white or black pepper
1-1/4 cups of cream

Sauté onion, bay leaf and parsley in butter stirring often until onion is softened but not brown. Add mushrooms, then stir in flour. Gradually stir in wine and chicken broth and bring to a boil. Sauce will be very thick. Cover pan and cook gently for about 15 minutes. Add salt and pepper to taste and beat vigorously. Remove bay leaf and parsley. Stir in the cream and heat gently. Do not boil.

TUNA TRIANGLES

1 full load of pasta dough made into triangles
2 (7 ounce) cans water-packed tuna, drained
1/3 cup green onion, finely chopped
2 garlic cloves, crushed
1-1/2 cups fresh white bread crumbs
grated peel of 1/2 lemon
1/3 cup freshly grated Parmesan cheese
salt and freshly ground black pepper to taste
about 1/2 cup milk
1 egg, beaten
freshly grated Parmesan cheese for garnish

Mash the tuna, then mix in the green onion, garlic and bread crumbs. Add the lemon peel, Parmesan cheese and salt and pepper to taste. Mix in just enough milk to bind the mixture. Make triangles according to instructions for making filled pasta in the Making Pasta chapter. You can assemble triangles as directed using the Ravioli Cutter for smaller shapes to make about 60 triangles or by hand method to make larger shapes. Beat the remaining egg. Be sure to brush bottom layer of dough with egg before placing stuffing on it and then covering with the top layer of dough. Pinch the edges of the dough together to seal. Cook the triangles until al dente. Do this in batches if necessary, then drain the pasta. Serve the triangles in White Wine Sauce (see previous page) or the Marinara or Alfredo Sauce from the Sauces Chapter. Pass freshly grated Parmesan cheese at the table.

SIRLOIN STUFFED CANNELLONI

1 full load of pasta dough made into cannelloni
1 pound ground sirloin
salt and pepper to taste
3 large eggs
1/2 cup grated Parmesan cheese
1/2 cup bread crumbs
1 tablespoon chopped parsley or flakes
2 cups of marinara sauce (see recipe page 46)

Make cannelloni according to instructions for cutting pasta shapes in the Making Pasta chapter. You'll need about 18 squares, 4 x 4-inch. Cook the pieces of pasta, a few at a time if necessary, until al dente. Drain and rinse under cold water, then lay out on double-thick paper towels. Preheat the oven to 350° F. To make stuffing, mix meat, eggs, 1/4 cup cheese, breadcrumbs, and parsley together until well-blended. Add salt and pepper to taste. Place some of the sirloin mixture on a piece of pasta, then roll it up into a neat tube. Place cannelloni, seam side down, in shallow ovenproof baking dish that has a little marinara sauce covering the bottom. Repeat with the remaining pasta and filling. Ladle remaining marinara sauce over the cannelloni, then sprinkle with the remaining cheese. Cover with foil and bake for 1 hour.

PASTA STUFFED WITH RICOTTA

1 full load of pasta dough made into ravioli OR
your choice of stuffed pasta
3 cups Ricotta cheese
2 or 3 eggs (depending on dryness of cheese)
3/4 cup freshly grated Parmesan cheese
1/4 cup parsley, chopped
salt and pepper to taste
1 egg, beaten for assembling ravioli
2 cups of marinara sauce (see recipe page 46)
freshly grated Parmesan cheese for garnish

Mix Ricotta, eggs, Parmesan and parsley in a bowl until smooth. Salt and pepper to taste and set aside. Make ravioli according to instructions for making filled pasta in the Making Pasta chapter. You can assemble ravioli as directed using the Ravioli Cutter for smaller shapes to make about 80 ravioli or by hand method to make larger shapes. Beat the remaining egg. Be sure to brush bottom layer of dough with egg before placing stuffing on it and then covering with the top layer of dough. Pinch the edges of the dough together to seal or you can use the tines of a fork to make a regular pattern. Cook the ravioli until al dente. Do this in batches if necessary, then drain the pasta. Serve covered with marinara sauce and top with grated cheese.

VARIATIONS: This stuffing works equally as well for making cannelloni, manicotti, tortellini, cappelletti, or any other fancy shape you can make by hand.

TORTELLINI IN PARMESAN CREAM SAUCE

1 full load of pasta dough made into tortellini

SPINACH AND RICOTTA FILLING
*1/2 pound fresh spinach, finely chopped
and cooked
1-1/2 cups ricotta cheese
1/3 cup freshly grated Parmesan cheese
1-1/2 cups fresh white bread crumbs
1/8 teaspoon of dried thyme
1 teaspoon dried marjoram
1/8 teaspoon of grated nutmeg
salt and freshly ground black pepper to taste
2 eggs, beaten*

BEEF FILLING
*2 tablespoons olive oil
1 small onion, finely chopped
2 garlic cloves, crushed
1/2 teaspoon dried marjoram
1/2 teaspoon thyme, chopped
1/4 teaspoon ground coriander
salt and freshly ground black pepper to taste
1/2 pound ground sirloin
1/2 cup lean bacon, cooked and crumbled
2 eggs, beaten
1/2 cup grated Parmesan cheese
1/2 cup bread crumbs*

BEEF AND PORK FILLING
*3/4 pound beef
1/4 pound pork*

144

2 eggs, beaten
1/2 cup bread crumbs
1/4 cup grated Parmesan cheese
1/4 cup water
1 clove garlic, finely minced
1/4 cup parsley, finely minced, OR
1/4 cup cooked spinach, finely minced
salt and freshly ground black pepper to taste

Choose cheese or one of the meat fillings or half the quantities for each filling recipe and serve a combination of two. To make either filling mix all ingredients in a bowl until smooth. Make tortellini according to instructions for making filled pasta in the Making Pasta chapter. Cook the tortellini until al dente. Do this in batches if necessary, then drain the pasta. Toss with butter. Serve covered with cream sauce (see recipe below). Place tortellini onto serving plates and spoon sauce over each dish.

VARIATIONS: These stuffings work equally as well for making cannelloni, manicotti, ravioli, cappelletti, or other fancy hand-cut shapes.

CREAM SAUCE

2 cups heavy cream
1/2 cup grated Parmesan cheese
2 tablespoons butter or margarine, softened

Heat cream to boiling in a saucepan, adjusting heat to prevent cream from boiling over, until reduced to 1 cup, about 10 minutes. Stir in Parmesan cheese. Serve immediately over hot pasta.

SALMON-STUFFED SPINACH PASTA ROLL WITH RED PEPPER SAUCE

*1 full load of spinach pasta dough
made into oversized cannelloni*

ROASTED PEPPER SAUCE
*6 red bell peppers
4 cups whipping cream
salt
ground cayenne pepper*

SALMON FILLING
*3/4 pound fresh salmon fillet
salt
freshly ground white pepper
2 eggs
1 cup plus 2 tablespoons whipping cream
red bell pepper sliced paper thin for garnish
smelt eggs or caviar for garnish (optional)*

Make oversized cannelloni according to instructions for cutting pasta shapes in the Making Pasta chapter. You'll need about 5 rectangles, 6 x 8-inch. Cook the pieces of pasta, a few at a time if necessary, until al dente. Drain and rinse under cold water, then lay out on paper towels. Preheat the oven to 400°F. To make the sauce, roast the whole peppers over charcoal or a gas flame or place under a broiler, turning several times, until the skin is charred all over. Cover with a paper towel to cool for about 10 minutes. Rub away charred skin with your fingertips. Cut peppers in half, seed, and coarsely chop. In a saucepan, com-

146

bine the peppers and the 4 cups cream over medium heat and cook until the cream is reduced by half, 10 to 15 minutes. Transfer to a food processor or blender and purée until smooth. Season to taste with salt and cayenne pepper. Set aside. Reheat just before serving. To make filling, make sure ingredients are well chilled before preparing. Purée the salmon in a food processor or blender until as smooth as possible. Add salt and pepper to taste, and the eggs. Blend until well mixed then slowly add the 1 cup plus 2 tablespoons cream and purée until very smooth. Evenly spread salmon mixture over each sheet of pasta tapering off toward the edges. Starting on a short side, roll up each pasta sheet jelly-roll style. Repeat with the remaining pasta and filling. Wrap each roll in a double layer of cheesecloth and tie with cotton string in several places. In a wide pan, bring to a simmer in enough water to cover the pasta rolls. Add the rolls and simmer for 20 minutes. Transfer the rolls to a wire rack set over a tray to drain and rest for about 10 minutes. Unwrap the pasta and cut into 1-inch-wide slices. Rinse knife between each cut to prevent pasta color from bleeding onto the filling. To serve, spoon a pool of the reheated pepper sauce onto each preheated plate. Top with slices of pasta roll and garnish with sweet pepper and smelt eggs or caviar (if used). Serve immediately.

VEGETABLE CANNELLONI

1 full load of pasta dough made into cannelloni
1 cup mozzarella cheese, grated

LEEK AND SPINACH FILLING
2 teaspoons olive oil
1 clove garlic, crushed
3 whole green onions, finely chopped
3 leeks, thinly sliced
1 red pepper, thinly sliced
1 pound fresh spinach, chopped
1 cup ricotta cheese, drained
1 (10 ounce) can creamed sweet corn
2 teaspoons ground paprika

TOMATO SAUCE
1 teaspoon olive oil
1 onion, chopped
14 ounces canned tomato pureé
2 tablespoons dry white wine

Make cannelloni according to instructions for cutting pasta shapes in the Making Pasta chapter. You'll need about 18 squares, 4 x 4-inches. Cook the pieces of pasta, a few at a time if necessary, until al dente. Drain and rinse under cold water, then lay out on double-thick paper towels. Preheat the oven to 350° F. To make filling, heat oil in a frying pan over a medium heat. Add garlic, green onions and leeks and cook, stirring frequently, for 4 minutes or until leeks are soft. Add red pepper and spinach and cook, stirring frequently, for 3 minutes or until spinach wilts. Drain off liquid. Transfer vegetable mixture to a large bowl, add ricotta cheese, sweet corn and paprika and mix well to combine. Spoon filling into cannelloni tubes and place tubes side-by-side in a large, greased ovenproof dish. Set aside. To make sauce, heat oil in a saucepan over a medium heat. Add onion and cook, stirring frequently, for 3 minutes or until onion is soft. Stir in tomato pureé and wine, and simmer for 4 minutes. Pour sauce over cannelloni tubes, sprinkle with mozzarella cheese and bake for 40 minutes or until pasta is tender and cheese is golden.

SHRIMP WON TON

1 full load of Chinese egg noodle pasta
made into won tons
1 pound shelled, de-veined shrimps
2 tablespoons sesame oil
2 cloves garlic, chopped
1 teaspoon fresh ginger, chopped
6 water chestnuts, chopped
4 green onions, chopped
2 tablespoons corn flour
salt and pepper to taste

Cook the shrimps in oil for about 5 minutes. Let cool, then chop finely. Combine the rest of the ingredients in a bowl and mix well. Make won tons according to instructions for making filled pasta in the Making Pasta chapter. Place a single layer of dumplings in a steamer and cook for about 10 minutes. Oil the steamer rack if it is made of metal. Repeat until all of the dumplings are ready. Serve with hot Chinese mustard.

POTATO AND CHEESE PIEROGI

FILLING
6 medium potatoes
1 large onion, chopped
1/3 pound farmer or cottage cheese
3 tablespoons butter or margarine
salt and pepper to taste

PIEROGI DOUGH
2 pasta measuring cups all purpose flour
1/2 to 3/4 cup sour cream
1 egg

Clean and peel the potatoes, cut them into quarters, and place them in a pot with just enough water to cover them. Cover the pot and boil the potatoes for 20 to 40 minutes, until tender. Drain them as soon as they are done. While the potatoes are cooking make a full load of pierogi dough using the above ingredients. Make pierogi shapes according to the instructions for halfmoon ravioli in the Making Pasta chapter. Sheets of pasta dough should be about 1/8 inch thick, cut into 2 or 3-inch circles. Mash the potatoes while they are still warm. Fry the onion in the butter. Combine the potatoes, onion, and cheese in a bowl and mix well, adding salt and pepper to taste. Drop about 1 tablespoon of filling onto the center of each round. Moisten the exposed dough with water and fold each circle in half. Seal the open edges of the semicircle by pressing them together. Boil the pierogi for 5 to 8 minutes in salted water. Drain and serve them with melted butter and sour cream.

Eggplant Pillows

1 full load of pasta dough made into cannelloni
2 small eggplants
salt and freshly ground black pepper
4-6 tablespoons olive oil
3 large slices lean cooked ham
10 sage leaves
10 slices Mozzarella cheese
2 large onions, thinly sliced
1 pound ripe tomatoes, peeled and sliced
1/2 cup soft cheese with garlic and herbs
1 cup fine dry white bread crumbs
4 tablespoons freshly grated Parmesan cheese

Make cannelloni according to instructions for cutting pasta shapes in the Making Pasta chapter. You'll need about 10 rectangles, 4 x 6-inches. Cook the pieces of pasta, a few at a time if necessary, until al dente. Drain and rinse under cold water, then lay out on paper towels. Trim the eggplants and cut 20 slices. Layer these in a strainer with a little salt, place over a bowl, then leave to stand for 30 minutes. Rinse well and dry on paper towels. Heat some olive oil in a skillet and brown the eggplant slices on both sides, adding more oil as necessary. Cut the ham into ten pieces. Make 10 eggplant sandwiches by placing a piece of ham, sage leaf and slice of Mozzarella between two slices of eggplant. Place an eggplant sandwich in the center of each pasta rectangle and fold the pasta over it to make a neat package. Repeat with the remaining ingredients. Set the oven at 350°F. Heat any remaining olive oil. Add the onions and

15-20 minutes, until softened. Spread the onions in the base of an ovenproof dish. Top with the tomatoes and salt and pepper to taste. Arrange the eggplant pillows on top, with the ends of the pasta dough underneath. Dot the tops of the packages with the soft cheese, spreading it slightly. Mix the bread crumbs and Parmesan, then sprinkle some over the top of each package. Cover with greased foil and bake for 20 minutes, then remove the foil and cook for an additional 10 minutes.

Seafood

Chapter 10

Each recipe serves 4 to 6 people
unless otherwise indicated.

Most of the recipes in this book
call for a full load of fresh pasta dough
made into a specific pasta shape using
the Automatic Pasta Maker.

All of the pasta dough recipes can be
mixed and rolled by hand and many of
the shapes can be cut by hand if you
don't have a machine.

You may substitute
16 ounces of dried pasta
for a full load of fresh pasta.

SPINACH FETTUCCINE WITH SCALLOPS

1 full load of spinach pasta dough
made into fettuccine
3 tablespoons butter or margarine
3 tablespoons olive oil
1 pound bay scallops
1/2 green bell pepper, seeded and diced
1 large tomato, seeded and diced
5 green onions, chopped
12 mushrooms, sliced
2-1/2 cups heavy cream
1/3 cup freshly grated Parmesan cheese
6 ounces Boursin garlic cheese
salt and freshly ground black pepper to taste

Make fettuccine and set aside. In large skillet over moderate heat, melt butter with oil. Add scallops and sauté 2-3 minutes or until opaque. Stir in green pepper, tomato, green onions and mushrooms. Sauté for 4 minutes. Add cream and Parmesan cheese and stir until well blended. Reduce heat and simmer until sauce thickens, about 8-10 minutes. Add Boursin cheese and stir until blended. Cook fettuccine until al dente and drain. In heated serving dish, toss warm fettuccine with scallop mixture. Add salt and pepper to taste. Serve immediately.

LINGUINE WITH WHITE CLAM SAUCE

1 full load of pasta dough made into linguine
2 cloves garlic, minced
1/3 cup butter or margarine
3 tablespoons all-purpose flour
2-1/2 cups bottled clam juice
1/4 cup fresh parsley, minced
1-1/2 teaspoons dried thyme
salt and freshly ground black pepper to taste
3 cups fresh minced clams OR
4 (6-1/4 ounce) cans minced clams

Make linguine and set aside. In a large skillet, sauté garlic in butter over medium-high heat for 1 minute. Whisk in flour until smooth and add clam juice. Whisk until mixed. Add parsley, thyme, salt and pepper. Reduce heat and simmer for 12 minutes or until sauce is reduced by 1/3. The secret of this sauce is reducing the clam juice so the flavor is intensified. Add clams and heat through. Meanwhile, cook linguine until al dente, drain and place in a heated serving dish. Pour sauce over linguine and toss gently. Serve immediately.

ANGEL HAIR PASTA WITH BASIL AND CRAB

1 full load of pasta dough made into angel hair
1/2 pound butter or margarine
3 tablespoons chopped shallots
2 tablespoons fresh basil, minced
3 tablespoons fresh parsley, minced
3 (16-ounce) cans peeled and chopped
tomatoes, drained
1/2 cup dry white wine
1-1/2 pounds crabmeat OR
imitation crabmeat
freshly grated Parmesan cheese

Make angel hair and set aside. In large skillet, melt butter and sauté shallots, basil and parsley for 2-3 minutes. Stir in tomatoes and heat to boiling. Cook sauce until reduced by half. Add wine and simmer 5 minutes. Meanwhile, cook angel hair until al dente, drain and place in a heated serving dish. Add crabmeat to sauce and simmer another 2-3 minutes. Remove from heat. Pour sauce over angel hair and toss gently. Serve immediately. Serve with Parmesan cheese.

GARLIC/BASIL TAGLIATELLE WITH SHRIMP

1 full load of garlic/basil pasta dough
made into tagliatelle
4 tablespoons butter or margarine
1 pound large shrimp, peeled and de-veined
8 Roma tomatoes, peeled and diced
(about 2 1/2 cups)
1/2 pound mushrooms, sliced
1/4 cup brandy
2 tablespoons minced fresh basil or
1 teaspoon dried basil
1/2 teaspoon salt
1/2 teaspoon freshly ground black pepper
1-1/2 cups heavy cream
1 cup freshly grated Parmesan cheese

Make tagliatelle and set aside. In large skillet, melt butter over medium-high heat and sauté shrimp for 2-3 minutes or until shrimp are firm and opaque. Remove shrimp; set aside. Add tomatoes and mushrooms to skillet and sauté for 5 minutes. Stir in brandy, basil, salt and pepper. Add cream and cook until sauce is reduced by 1/3, about 5-7 minutes. Meanwhile, cook tagliatelle until al dente, drain and place in a heated serving dish. Add Parmesan to sauce and stir. Reduce heat to low and add shrimp to sauce. Stir for 1-2 minutes to heat shrimp. Remove from heat. Pour sauce over tagliatelle and toss gently. Serve immediately.

SEAFOOD PASTA EXTRAORDINAIRÉ

TOMATO SAUCE
6 cloves garlic, minced
3 tablespoons olive oil
4 (28 ounce) cans stewed Italian tomatoes,
crushed
2 tablespoons sugar
1 cup fresh basil, minced
1/4 teaspoon ground white pepper

1 full load of pasta dough made into vermicelli
4 cloves garlic, minced
3 tablespoons olive oil
1 pound large fresh shrimp, peeled
and de-veined
1 pound sea scallops, muscle removed
freshly grated Parmesan cheese (optional)

In 8-quart saucepan, sauté 6 cloves garlic in oil until golden. Add the tomatoes, sugar, basil and pepper. Simmer uncovered over low heat for 1 to 1-1/2 hours. Make vermicelli and set aside. In large skillet, sauté 4 cloves garlic in oil over medium heat for 2 minutes. Add shrimp and scallops and sauté for 3 minutes or until shrimp are pink and scallops opaque. Do not overcook. Meanwhile, cook vermicelli until al dente, drain and place in a heated serving dish. Finally, add seafood to tomato sauce. Heat through, about 1-2 minutes. Pour sauce over pasta and serve with Parmesan cheese.

FETTUCCINE WITH SCALLOPS, RED PEPPER, AND ANCHOVY SAUCE

1 full load of pasta dough made into fettuccine
6 tablespoons olive oil
2 medium red bell peppers (about 12 ounces),
seeded and cut into 1/4-inch strips
2 garlic cloves, crushed
4 anchovy fillets, finely chopped
12 ounces bay scallops **OR**
sea scallops, halved or quartered
1/4 cup thinly sliced green onions, both
white and green parts

Make fettuccini and set aside. Cut the red pepper strips about the same width as the fettuccini. Heat oil in a medium skillet and add red peppers. Sauté over medium-high heat 5 minutes, or until peppers begin to blister and brown on the edges. Stir in the garlic and anchovy fillets. Sauté 2 minutes, stirring, to dissolve the anchovies. Add the scallops then sauté over high heat until just cooked through about 3 minutes. Adjust heat so that the other ingredients don't brown. Meanwhile, cook fettuccini until al dente, drain and place in a heated serving dish. Toss with the scallop mixture and sprinkle with sliced green onions before serving.

SPAGHETTI WITH ANCHOVIES

1 full load of pasta dough made into spaghetti
salt
olive oil
1 garlic clove, sliced
4 slices firm white bread, minced
1 (2 ounce) can anchovies in oil,
drained and mashed
1 (13 ounce) jar pimento-stuffed olives, chopped
1/4 cup parsley, chopped
1/3 cup freshly grated Parmesan cheese

Make spaghetti, cook al dente and drain. Reserve 1/3 cup pasta cooking water. Return spaghetti to pot to keep warm. Meanwhile, in a 10-inch skillet over medium heat, add 1 tablespoon hot olive oil and cook garlic until golden. Remove garlic with slotted spoon and set aside for garnish. In hot oil remaining in skillet over medium heat, cook bread and 1/4 teaspoon salt until bread crumbs are lightly toasted, shaking skillet frequently. To serve, toss spaghetti in a heated serving bowl with reserved pasta cooking water, anchovies, olives, parsley, and 2 tablespoons olive oil. Sprinkle with toasted bread crumbs and Parmesan cheese.

FUSILLI WITH CHILI OCTOPUS

1 full load of spinach dough made into fusilli
2 pounds baby octopus OR
calamari (squid) rings, cleaned

MARINADE
1 tablespoon sesame oil
1 tablespoon grated fresh ginger
2 tablespoons lime juice
2 tablespoons sweet chili sauce

TOMATO SAUCE
2 teaspoons olive oil
3 green onions, sliced diagonally
14 ounces canned tomato purée

To make marinade, place sesame oil, ginger, lime juice and chili sauce in a large bowl and mix. Add octopus or squid, toss to coat, cover and marinate in the refrigerator for 3-4 hours. Make fusilli, cook al dente, drain, and set aside to keep warm. To make sauce, heat oil in a saucepan over medium heat. Add green onions and cook, stirring, for 1 minute. Stir in tomato purée, bring to simmering and cook for 4 minutes. Cook octopus or squid under a preheated broiler for 5-7 minutes or until tender. Add octopus to sauce and toss to combine. Spoon octopus mixture over hot pasta and toss again. Serve immediately.

SEAFOOD FETTUCCINE

1 half load each of spinach and tomato
pasta made into fettuccine
1 tablespoon olive oil
1 onion, sliced
1 red pepper, diced
1 clove garlic, crushed
1 red chili, seeded and finely chopped
1/2 teaspoon ground cumin
1/2 teaspoon ground coriander
14 ounces canned tomatoes,
undrained and mashed
1/4 cup dry white wine
1 tablespoon tomato paste
5 ounces calamari, cut into rings
5 ounces cleaned fresh mussels in shells
1 pound large prawns, peeled and deveined
4 tablespoons finely chopped fresh coriander
freshly ground black pepper to taste

Make fettuccine and set aside. Heat oil in a large saucepan and cook onion, pepper, garlic, chili, cumin and ground coriander until onion is soft. Add tomatoes, wine and tomato paste and cook over a medium heat for 30 minutes or until sauce reduces and thickens. Add calamari to sauce and cook for 5 minutes or until just tender. Add mussels and prawns and cook for 4-5 minutes longer. Meanwhile, cook fettuccini until al dente, drain and place in a heated serving dish. Add half of the fresh coriander to sauce and season with pepper. Spoon sauce over cooked fettuccine and sprinkle with remaining fresh coriander. Serve immediately.

CAVIAR FETTUCCINE

1 full load of pasta dough made into fettuccine
1/4 cup olive oil
4 cloves garlic, crushed
4 tablespoons fresh chives, finely snipped
*6 tablespoons each red and black caviar **OR***
substitute red and black lumpfish roe
4 hard-boiled eggs, chopped
1/2 cup sour cream

Make fettuccini, cook until al dente, drain and place in a heated serving dish. Heat oil in a large frying pan and cook garlic over a low heat for 3-4 minutes. Add fettuccine, chives, red and black caviar, and eggs to pan. Toss to combine. Top with sour cream and serve immediately.

BAKED MACARONI AND TUNA

1 full load of pasta dough made into macaroni
1 pound pimiento cheese, divided in half
2 (7 ounce) cans tuna, drained
2 tablespoons flour
1 quart milk

Make macaroni, cook until al dente, drain and set aside. In double boiler, heat milk and slowly add half of the cheese. Add flour and stir until thickened. Add tuna and mix thoroughly with sauce, then add macaroni. Pour in greased baking pan. Lay the remaining cheese, cut in strips, over top. Bake for 30 minutes at 350°F.

Shrimp Alfredo

1 full load of pasta dough made into fettuccini
1/4 cup butter or margarine
1 pound medium shrimp, peeled and de-veined
1 tablespoon minced green onions
2 cloves garlic, minced
5 egg yolks
1-1/2 cups half and half
1-1/2 cups freshly grated Parmesan cheese
1/4 cup fresh parsley, minced
1/2 teaspoon salt
freshly ground black pepper to taste

Make fettuccini, cook until al dente, drain and place in a heated serving dish. In a large skillet, melt butter and sauté shrimp, green onions and garlic over moderate heat for 3-4 minutes, or until shrimp are firm and opaque. Remove pan from heat. Stir warm fettuccine into shrimp mixture. In medium bowl, beat egg yolks, half and half and Parmesan. Add egg yolk mixture to shrimp mixture and cook over moderate heat until sauce thickens, about 3-4 minutes. Do not boil. Stir in parsley, salt and pepper. Serve immediately.

SPAGHETTI MILANESE

1 full load of pasta dough made into spaghetti
2 cups bread crumbs
olive oil
1 medium head cauliflower
3 to 4 cloves garlic, minced
1 small can anchovies, cut in pieces
1/4 teaspoon Cayenne pepper (optional)
1/4 cup sugar (optional)
2 cans Milanese paste
salt and freshly ground black pepper to taste
1/3 cup olive oil
3 (6-ounce) cans tomato paste

Oil a heavy skillet. Add bread crumbs. Cook and stir constantly over medium heat until lightly browned. Set aside to use for topping. Break cauliflower in small florets. Boil in salted water until partly cooked. Drain. Reserve water cauliflower was boiled in. Set aside. Meanwhile, make spaghetti, cook al dente, drain, and set aside to keep warm. Sauté garlic in 1/3 cup oil until light brown. Add can of anchovies. Stir until dissolved, about 3 minutes. Add tomato paste and about 2-1/2 quarts of water that cauliflower was boiled in. Add salt, pepper and sugar (optional). Simmer over low heat for about 1-1/2 hours or until thickened. Add cauliflower and Milanese paste. Salt and pepper to taste. Toss sauce with cooked spaghetti and serve with bread crumb topping instead of cheese.

LOBSTER WITH MARINARA SAUCE

1 full load of pasta dough made into spaghetti
1/2 cup olive oil or vegetable oil
6 (5 ounces each) frozen rock lobster tails, thawed
4 cloves garlic, finely minced
1 cup chopped onions
1 (2 pound-3 ounce) can plum tomatoes,
undrained, mashed with a fork to a pulp
1/2 teaspoon oregano
1/2 teaspoon basil

Make spaghetti and set aside. To make sauce, sauté onions and garlic in hot oil until tender, but not brown, in large saucepan. Add tomatoes, stir and let come to a boil. Lower heat and boil gently for 30 minutes. Add basil and oregano. Cook for another 15 minutes. Meanwhile, cut under-shells of lobsters lengthwise, leaving top shell intact. Remove lobster meat whole and wash thoroughly. Add lobster meat to sauce. Simmer for about 30 minutes, covered. Meanwhile cook spaghetti al dente, drain, and arrange in center of a heated serving platter. Remove lobster tails from sauce then pour sauce over cooked spaghetti. Arrange lobster meat around spaghetti with sauce. Serve immediately.

SCALLOPS WITH SPINACH AND CUCUMBERS

1 full load of pasta dough made into linguine
4 tablespoons unsalted butter
5 large shallots, minced
1 (12-ounce) package frozen chopped spinach,
thawed and squeezed dry
1/2 teaspoon salt
1-1/2 cups cucumber, peeled, seeded and chopped
1-1/4 cups heavy cream
1/2 teaspoon salt
1/4 teaspoon ground nutmeg
1/4 teaspoon crushed red pepper flakes
1 pound sea scallops, cut horizontally into thirds
2/3 cup freshly grated Parmesan cheese

Make linguine and set aside. In large skillet, melt butter over medium heat. Sauté shallots for 3 minutes. Add spinach and 1/2 teaspoon salt and cook, stirring frequently, until wilted, about 2 minutes. Add cucumber and cook over medium heat until cucumber softens, about another 2 minutes. Stir in cream, 1/2 teaspoon salt, nutmeg and red pepper flakes. Boil. Reduce heat and simmer until sauce thickens about 6 minutes. Gently mix scallops into heated sauce and cook until just opaque, about 30 seconds; do not overcook. Meanwhile, make spaghetti, cook al dente, drain, put into a large, heated serving dish. Toss warm linguine with scallop mixture. Sprinkle with Parmesan and serve immediately.

AVOCADO AND SHRIMP FETTUCINE

1 full load of pasta dough made into linguine
6 tablespoon butter or margarine
2 teaspoons minced garlic
1/2 cup minced fresh parsley
1 pound shrimp, peeled and deveined
1/2 cup dry vermouth or white wine
1 cup heavy cream
1/2 cup freshly grated Parmesan cheese
pinch of crushed red pepper flakes
salt and freshly ground black pepper to taste
2 medium avocados, peeled, pitted and cubed

Make linguine and set aside. In large skillet, heat 2 tablespoons butter over medium-high heat. Add minced garlic and cook for 1 minute. Add parsley, shrimp and vermouth and cook for 2 minutes, stirring constantly, until shrimp turn pink. Do not overcook. Transfer shrimp mixture to small bowl. In the same skillet, heat 4 more tablespoons butter until melted. Reduce heat to low and add cream, Parmesan and red pepper flakes. Cook for 3 minutes, stirring constantly, until cheese melts and sauce is smooth. Stir in salt and pepper to taste. Meanwhile, cook linguine until al dente, drain, and transfer to a heated serving bowl. Add cream sauce, shrimp mixture, and avocado and toss gently to coat thoroughly.

LINGUINE IMPERIAL

1 full load of pasta dough made into linguine
1/4 pound butter or margarine
1 tablespoon olive oil
2 cloves garlic, minced
1/4 cup minced fresh parsley
2 tablespoons minced fresh basil or
2 teaspoons dried basil
1-1/2 cups fresh green beans, julienne sliced
1-1/2 pounds fresh crabmeat OR
imitation crabmeat
4 egg yolks, lightly beaten
1/2 cup freshly grated Parmesan cheese
1 cup heavy cream
1/2 teaspoon salt

Make linguine and set aside. Prepare green beans and cook in a microwave or steam until they are just tender to the bite. In a large skillet, heat together butter and oil. Saute garlic, parsley and basil over low heat for 5 minutes. Stir in crabmeat and cook for 2 minutes. Remove from heat. Meanwhile, cook linguine until al dente, drain, and transfer to a heated serving platter. In small bowl, thoroughly combine egg yolks, Parmesan, cream and salt. Toss warm linguine with egg mixture. Add crabmeat mixture and toss gently until combined. Serve immediately.

Poultry

Chapter 11

Each recipe serves 4 to 6 people
unless otherwise indicated.

───── ───── ───── ─────

Most of the recipes in this book
call for a full load of fresh pasta dough
made into a specific pasta shape using
the Automatic Pasta Maker.

───── ───── ───── ─────

All of the pasta dough recipes can be
mixed and rolled by hand and many of
the shapes can be cut by hand if you
don't have a machine.

───── ───── ───── ─────

You may substitute
16 ounces of dried pasta
for a full load of fresh pasta.

FETTUCCINE VERDE WITH CHICKEN

*1 full load spinach pasta dough
made into fettuccine
3 tablespoons olive oil
1 large onion, thinly sliced
1-1/2 cups mushrooms, thinly sliced
2 cloves garlic, minced or pressed
1/4 cup butter or margarine
1 (3 ounce) package thinly sliced ham,
cut into julienne strips
1 large tomato, chopped
1 teaspoon dry basil
3 cups shredded cooked chicken
1-1/4 cups whipping cream
1/2 cup fresh parsley, chopped
2/3 cup dry white wine or dry sherry
1/8 teaspoon ground nutmeg
salt and freshly ground black pepper to taste
1/2 cup freshly grated Parmesan cheese*

Make fettuccine and set aside. Heat oil in a wide frying pan over medium-high heat. Add onion and cook, stirring often, until lightly browned. Add mushrooms and continue to cook, stirring, until lightly browned. Add garlic, butter, ham, tomato, and basil. Bring to a gentle boil, then reduce heat and boil gently, uncovered, for 5 minutes. Meanwhile cook fettuccine until al dente, drain and transfer to a heated serving platter. While fettuccine is cooking, add chicken, cream, parsley, wine, and nutmeg to mushroom-ham mixture. Mix gently until hot, then add to fettuccine and toss. Season to taste with salt and pepper. Serve with Parmesan cheese.

CHICKEN FLORENTINE

1 full load of pasta dough made into bowties
1 pound fresh spinach, chopped
2-1/2 teaspoons salt
3 large whole chicken breasts, de-boned,
skinned, split in half lengthwise
1/4 teaspoon white pepper
1/3 cup all-purpose flour
1/3 cup butter
3 tablespoons olive oil
2 tablespoons freshly squeezed lemon juice
1 cup chopped onion
3 garlic cloves, pressed
1 cup half and half
2/3 cup dry vermouth
2/3 cup freshly grated Parmesan cheese

Place washed spinach in a colander. Sprinkle with 2 teaspoons salt. Let stand 1/2 hour. Meanwhile make bowties according to the instructions for making cut pasta shapes in the Making Pasta chapter and set aside. Squeeze spinach to remove excess water. Flatten chicken by pounding lightly between 2 pieces of waxed paper. Sprinkle with remaining 1/2 teaspoon salt and pepper. Coat lightly in flour. Heat butter and olive oil over medium heat in a large skillet. Add chicken and brown on both sides until golden, about 10 minutes. Sprinkle with lemon juice. Remove chicken from skillet. Set aside. Add onion and garlic to pan drippings. Sauté until golden. Add spinach. Sauté until tender, about 5 minutes. Add half and half and vermouth. Stir in half of the Parmesan

cheese. Add chicken. Cover and heat through. Set aside. Cook bowties until al dente, drain and transfer to a heated serving platter. Sprinkle pasta with the remaining 1/4 cup grated Parmesan cheese. Toss well. Serve Chicken Florentine over hot cooked bowties.

DUCK LASAGNE

1 full load of pasta dough made into lasagne
Bolognese-Style Meat Sauce (see recipe page 45)
3 tablespoons olive oil
1 duck (about 5 pounds), cut into pieces,
excess fat removed
White Sauce (see recipe page 140)
2 cups freshly grated Parmesan cheese
1/4 cup (1/2 stick) unsalted butter

Prepare the meat sauce and simmer for 1 hour. Meanwhile, heat the oil in a sauté pan or skillet over medium-high heat. Add the duck and brown all over. Wrap the duck in cheesecloth and immerse in the meat sauce. Continue to simmer, turning the duck several times, until the duck is very tender, about 2 hours. Transfer the duck to a plate to cool, then remove the cheesecloth. Discard skin and bones. Shred duck meat and return it to the simmering meat sauce. Meanwhile, prepare the White Sauce as described and set aside. Make lasagne and cook a few at a time until al dente and drain. Rinse each noodle under cold

running water, then squeeze them with your hands and lay them on a paper towel. Pat dry with another towel. Preheat oven to 450°F. Grease the bottom and sides of a 12 x 9-inch baking pan, preferably with straight sides and square corners. To assemble, spread a thin layer of the meat sauce on the bottom of the pan. Add a single layer of lasagna noodles to completely cover the bottom of the pan. Spread a thin layer of the meat sauce over the noodles, cover with a thin layer of the White Sauce, then lightly sprinkle with the cheese. Continue layering in this way until all the ingredients have been used, ending with a layer of White Sauce and a topping of cheese. Dot with the butter and bake until the top forms a lightly golden crust, about 15 minutes. Remove from the oven and let stand about 10 minutes before serving.

BARBECUED CORNISH HEN WITH PAPPARDELLE IN MUSHROOM SAUCE

1 full load of pasta dough made into pappardelle
3 ounces sliced pancetta OR bacon, diced
1/2 cup olive oil
1 medium-size onion, thinly sliced
8 ounces mushrooms, quartered
2 cloves garlic, minced or pressed
8 medium-size Roma tomatoes, chopped
1/3 cup slivered fresh sage leaves or
2 teaspoons dry sage
1-1/4 cups dry white wine
5 Cornish hens
freshly ground black pepper to taste
fresh sage sprigs (optional)
lemon wedges (optional)

Make pappardelle and set aside. In a wide frying pan, cook pancetta over medium heat until crisp. Lift out, drain, and set aside. To pan drippings, add 1/4 cup of the oil, then onion and mushrooms. Increase heat to medium-high and cook, stirring often, until mushrooms are lightly browned about 5 minutes. Stir in garlic, tomatoes, slivered sage, and wine. Adjust heat so mixture boils gently. Cook uncovered, stirring occasionally, until tomatoes are soft and sauce is slightly thickened about 10 to 15 minutes. Meanwhile, remove necks and giblets of hens and reserve for other uses, if desired. Rinse hens and pat dry. Cut each in half, cutting through backbone and breastbone. Brush well on all sides with remaining olive oil and sprin-

177

kle with pepper. Grill over medium coals. Cook, turning several times, until meat near thighbone is no longer pink. Cut to test after about 30 to 40 minutes. Remove from grill and keep warm. Cook pappardelle until al dente, and drain. Add pancetta to tomato sauce; season to taste with salt. Add pasta and mix lightly, using 2 spoons. Transfer pasta to the center of a heated serving platter. Arrange hens around pasta mound. Garnish with sage sprigs and lemon wedges, if desired.

NOTE: You can substitute 8 quail for the Cornish hens if available. Just cut through the backbone skin side up and press firmly on a flat surface until bones crack slightly and birds lay flat. Place birds skin side up on a lightly greased grill 4 to 6 inches above a bed of hot coals. Cook, turning occasionally, until browned. Breast meat should be pink at the bone. Cut to test after about 8 to 10 minutes total time. Don't overcook as quail will dry out quickly.

TURKEY WITH TORTELLINI & ORANGES

1 full load of pasta dough made into meat
or cheese tortellini (see recipes in Stuffed
and Specialty chapter)
3 large oranges (about 1-1/2 pounds total)
7 cups regular-strength chicken broth
3 cups diced, cooked turkey OR chicken
2 teaspoons celery seeds
2 cups sour cream
1/4 cup chopped chives

Make tortellini and set aside. Using a vegetable peeler, cut a strip of peel (colored part only) 6 inches long and about 1 inch wide from one of the oranges. Cut strip into long, thin shreds and set aside. Then completely peel all 3 oranges, discarding peel and white membrane. Cut each orange crosswise into 6 slices; set slices aside. In a 5 to 6-quart pan, bring broth to a boil. Add tortellini and cook until al dente. Remove cooked tortellini with a slotted spoon and transfer to a heated serving platter. To broth in pan, add turkey or chicken, celery seeds, and orange peel shreds. Cook until meat is just heated through. Lift out meat and spoon over tortellini. Place sour cream in a small pan, then stir in 3 tablespoons of the chives and 1/2 cup of the hot broth (reserve remaining broth for other uses). Stir broth-sour cream mixture over low heat just until hot, then spoon over pasta and meat. Sprinkle with remaining 1 tablespoon chives and arrange orange slices around the edges of the serving platter.

179

SPAGHETTI WITH TURKEY PARMESAN

1 full load of pasta dough made into spaghetti
Tomato-Onion Sauce (recipe follows)
1 egg
1/2 cup soft bread crumbs
1-1/3 cups (about 7 ounces)
grated Parmesan cheese
1/2 teaspoon poultry seasoning
1 pound ground turkey
1 tablespoon butter or margarine
1 tablespoon olive oil
1/4 pound mozzarella cheese, sliced
Italian (flat-leaf) parsley sprigs (optional)

Make spaghetti and set aside. Prepare Tomato-Onion Sauce; keep warm over low heat. In a medium-size bowl, beat egg until blended. Add bread crumbs, 1/3 cup of the Parmesan cheese, and poultry seasoning; stir until blended. Add turkey; mix lightly until well combined. Shape turkey mixture into 4 patties, each about 4 inches in diameter. Melt butter and oil in a wide frying pan over medium-high heat. Add turkey patties and cook for about 8 minutes, turning once, until browned on both sides. Transfer patties to a shallow rimmed baking pan or broiler pan. Spread each patty with 2 tablespoons of the Tomato-Onion Sauce. Top patties with 1 slice of the mozzarella cheese and 1 tablespoon of the remaining Parmesan cheese. Just before broiling the patties, cook spaghetti until al dente, drain and remove to a heated serving platter. Meanwhile, broil turkey patties about 4 inches below heat until cheese is melted and

lightly browned about 3 to 4 minutes. Spoon remaining Tomato-Onion Sauce over spaghetti, then top with turkey patties. Garnish with parsley sprigs, if desired. Serve with remaining Parmesan cheese to add to taste.

TOMATO ONION SAUCE

2 tablespoons olive oil
1 medium onion
2 teaspoons dry oregano
1 bay leaf
1 clove garlic, minced or pressed
1 (15 ounce) can tomato sauce

Sauté onion in olive oil in a 2-quart pan over medium heat. Add oregano, bay leaf, and garlic. Stir in tomato sauce. Cover, reduce heat, and simmer for 20 minutes, stirring occasionally.

MEXICAN CHICKEN LASAGNE

CHILE-CHEESE FILLING
2 cups small-curd cottage cheese
2 eggs
1/3 cup chopped parsley
1 (4 ounce) can diced green chilies

1 full load of pasta dough made into lasagne
2 tablespoons olive oil or vegetable oil
1 medium-size onion, chopped
2 cloves garlic, minced or pressed
1 medium-size red bell pepper, chopped
2 (16 ounce) jars of mild chile salsa
1/2 teaspoon pepper
2 tablespoons chili powder
1 teaspoon ground cumin
4 cups cooked chicken, diced
1 cup sharp Cheddar cheese, shredded
1 cup jack cheese, shredded

Make lasagne noodles and set aside. Prepare Chile-Cheese Filling by combining all ingredients and mixing well. Set aside. Heat oil in a 4 to 5-quart pan over medium heat; add onion, garlic, and bell pepper. Cook, stirring often, until onion is soft but not brown for about 8 to 10 minutes. Add salsa, pepper, chili powder, and cumin; bring to a boil. Reduce heat and boil gently, uncovered, stirring often, until mixture is reduced to 1 quart or about 10 minutes. Meanwhile, cook lasagne until al dente, drain, rinse with cold water, and drain well again. Arrange half the lasagne over bottom of a 9 x 13-inch baking dish; spread with half the

the Chile-Cheese Filling, then cover with half the chicken. Spoon half the sauce over chicken; sprinkle with 1/2 cup each of the Cheddar and jack cheeses. Repeat layers, using remaining lasagne, filling, chicken, sauce, and shredded cheeses. (At this point, you may cover and refrigerate for up to 1 day.) Bake, covered, in a 375°F. oven until lasagna is bubbly and hot in center, about 45 to 50 minutes (55 minutes if refrigerated). Uncover and let stand for 5 minutes; cut into squares to serve.

CHICKEN WON TONS

1 full load Chinese Egg Noodle or Won Ton pasta
*dough made into won tons **OR***
60 won ton skins (ready-made)
1 pound uncooked chicken meat, skinless
1 tablespoon sesame oil
1 large, dried shitake mushroom
8 ounces Chinese leaves
2 green onions, chopped
1 teaspoon fresh ginger, chopped
1 clove garlic, chopped
1 tablespoon soy sauce
*vegetable oil for deep frying **OR***
chicken broth for boiling

Make won tons according to the instructions for making filled pasta in the Making Pasta chapter and set aside. Cook the chicken in the sesame oil until all of the meat loses its pink color. Allow it to cool and then dice it finely. Soak the mushroom in

183

warm water, then chop it. Clean, parboil, squeeze dry, and chop the Chinese leaves. Combine all of the ingredients except the won ton skins and the vegetable oil or chicken broth. Process the mixture in a food processor or blender. Place a teaspoon of filling in the center of each won ton wrapper. Fold the wrapper into a triangle and seal the edges. Flip the ends of the folded edge in toward the center of the triangle, and press the two points together. To deep fry, heat the vegetable oil to about 350°F. Drop in the won tons and cook until golden brown. To boil, heat the chicken broth to a rolling boil and drop in the won tons. When the water returns to a boil, reduce the heat and simmer the won tons for about 10 minutes. When they're done, the cooked won tons will float on the top of the broth. Serve with a variety of dipping sauces such as the traditional soy sauce-rice vinegar combination, a hot mustard sauce or an orange duck sauce.

CHICKEN ASPARAGUS WITH TARRAGON

*1 full load of pasta dough made into
fettuccini or linguine
2 large whole chicken breasts, de-boned,
skinned, and split in half lengthwise
1-1/2 teaspoons salt
3/4 teaspoon black pepper
1/4 cup all-purpose flour*

184

2 tablespoons olive oil
2 tablespoons butter or margarine
1 cup chopped onion
2 garlic cloves, pressed
1 pound asparagus, trimmed, cut diagonally
1/2 pound mushrooms, sliced
2 cups chopped fresh tomatoes
1/2 cup chicken broth
2 tablespoons chopped fresh tarragon or
1-1/2 teaspoons dried leaf tarragon
1 tablespoon balsamic vinegar
1 teaspoon sugar
1 cup freshly grated Parmesan cheese

Make fettuccine or linguine and set aside. Flatten chicken by pounding lightly between 2 pieces of waxed paper. Sprinkle with 1/2 teaspoon salt and 1/4 teaspoon pepper. Coat lightly in flour; set aside. Heat olive oil and butter in large skillet over medium heat. Sauté onion and garlic until onion is golden. Add chicken; cook on both sides until golden. Remove chicken; set aside. Add asparagus to drippings. Sauté 3 minutes. Add mushrooms and sauté 2 more minutes. Add tomatoes, chicken broth, tarragon, vinegar, sugar, remaining teaspoon of salt and remaining 1/2 teaspoon pepper. Cook about 8 minutes over low heat. Meanwhile, cook pasta until al dente, drain, and remove to a heated serving platter. Toss cooked pasta lightly with 1/4 cup of the Parmesan cheese. Stir remaining 3/4 cup Parmesan cheese into asparagus mixture. Cook and stir until thickened. Add chicken. Heat through. Pour chicken mixture immediately over pasta and serve.

HERBED CHICKEN DINNER

*1 full load of pasta dough made into spaghetti,
fusilli or linguine
1/4 cup olive or vegetable oil
juice of 1 lemon (about 2-1/2 tablespoons)
1 (2-1/2-pound) broiler-fryer chicken
6 tablespoons butter or margarine, melted
3/4 cup firmly packed fresh parsley leaves
1 small garlic clove, cut in half
1/2 teaspoon salt
1 teaspoon dried oregano
1/4 teaspoon dried basil
1/4 teaspoon dried thyme
freshly ground black pepper to taste*

Make your choice of pasta and set aside. In a small bowl, beat 1/4 cup oil and lemon juice with a fork. Pour over chicken pieces. Toss to coat evenly. Refrigerate for 1 hour. In a blender or food processor, combine butter, parsley leaves, garlic, 1/2 teaspoon salt, oregano, basil, thyme and pepper. Cover and blend at high speed a few seconds until parsley is minced. Set aside. Broil chicken pieces, skin-side up, about 8-inches from heat for 20 minutes or until golden brown. Turn and broil 20 minutes longer, until golden brown. During last 4 minutes of broiling, brush both sides of chicken pieces with 1/4 cup herb mixture. Cook pasta until al dente, drain, and remove to a heated serving platter. Toss with remaining herb mixture. Arrange chicken pieces at edges of casserole. Serve immediately.

CHICKEN KIEV

1 full load of pasta dough made into tagliatelle
1/4 pound butter
2 tablespoons chives, chopped
2 tablespoons fresh parsley, chopped
2 teaspoons dried tarragon
1/2 teaspoon dried rosemary, crushed
1/2 teaspoon dried oregano
garlic powder to taste
4 whole chicken breasts (about 2-1/2 pounds),
split, skinned, de-boned
1/4 cup flour
1 egg, beaten
1/2 cup dry bread crumbs
oil for deep-frying
salt to taste
freshly ground black pepper to taste
6 cups water
1 teaspoon salt
2 teaspoons vegetable oil
4 tablespoons soft butter
Grated Romano cheese

Make tagliatelle and set aside. You can make bread crumbs in your blender and dry them in a 250°F oven for 30 minutes. Or you can use commercial bread crumbs. Cut a stick of butter in half crosswise. Cut and shape each half into 8 rolls about 1/2 inch thick. In a small bowl, mix chives, parsley, tarragon, rosemary, oregano and garlic powder. Twirl butter rolls in mixed herbs. Place butter rolls in freezer 30 minutes. To flatten chicken breasts, pound them between 2 pieces of waxed

paper until they are 1/4 inch thick. Preheat oil in
deep fryer or heavy deep skillet to 350°F. At this
temperature a 1-inch cube of bread will turn gold-
en brown in 65 seconds. Place 1 frozen butter roll
in the center of each half breast. Carefully fold so
butter roll is completely enclosed. Secure with a
wooden pick. Roll chicken in flour, dip in beaten
egg, then roll in bread crumbs. Repeat with
remaining chicken and butter rolls. Deep-fry in oil
about 5 minutes until chicken is golden. Drain on
paper towels. Season with salt and pepper to
taste. Meanwhile cook tagliatelle until al dente,
drain, and remove to a large heated serving platter.
Toss cooked noodles with 4 tablespoons butter.
Sprinkle with Romano cheese. Arrange Chicken
Kiev around the platter and serve immediately.

TURKEY TETRAZZINI

1 full load of pasta dough made into vermicelli
1/2 pound fresh mushrooms, sliced
1/2 cup butter
3 tablespoons flour
1 teaspoon salt
1-1/2 cups half-and-half
1-1/2 cups chicken broth
2 egg yolks
1/2 cup dry white wine
3 cups cooked turkey, cubed
*1 cup Cheddar **OR** Swiss cheese, shredded*

Make vermicelli and set aside. Butter a 13 x 9-inch baking dish and set aside. In a medium skillet, sauté mushrooms in 2 tablespoons butter about 10 minutes and set aside. Melt remaining 4 tablespoons butter in a saucepan. Stir in flour and 1 teaspoon salt. Stir and cook until bubbly. Add half-and-half and broth. Cook and stir until thickened. In a small bowl, beat egg yolks. Gradually stir about 1 cup hot sauce into beaten egg yolks. Blend yolk mixture into hot sauce. Add wine and heat through. Cook vermicelli until al dente, drain and return pasta to dry cooking pot. Add 1-1/2 cups sauce to cooked vermicelli. Arrange mixture in prepared baking dish, making a well in the center. Add turkey and sauteed mushrooms to remaining sauce. Spoon into well. Sprinkle with shredded cheese. Cover and place in cold oven. Set temperature control at 400°F. Bake 20 minutes.

CHICKEN CARBONARA

1 full load of pasta dough made into linguine
1/2 cup pine nuts
4 slices bacon, chopped
4 eggs (room temperature)
1/2 cup freshly grated Parmesan cheese
1/3 cup whipping cream
1/4 cup chopped parsley
1/4 cup chopped fresh basil leaves or 2 table-
spoons dry basil
3 cloves garlic, minced or pressed
1-1/2 cups diced cooked chicken
1 to 2 tablespoons butter or margarine

Make linguine and set aside. Stir pine nuts in a wide frying pan over medium-low heat until lightly browned about 3 minutes. Remove from pan and set aside in a large bowl. Increase heat to medium, add bacon to pan and cook until brown about 7 minutes. Lift out bacon and place in the bowl with nuts. Reserve drippings in pan. Add eggs, cheese, cream, parsley, basil, garlic, and chicken to bacon and pine nuts. Beat until well mixed. To reserved bacon drippings in frying pan, add enough butter to make about 1/4 cup and melt in drippings over medium heat. Meanwhile cook linguine until al dente and drain. Add linguine to frying pan with bacon drippings then add the egg mixture. Mix lightly, using 2 forks, just until linguine is well coated and heated through. Serve immediately.

CHICKEN IN-A-POT

*1 full load of pasta dough made into
small macaroni
1 (2-1/2 pound) broiler-fryer chicken,
cut in pieces
1 tablespoon lemon juice
1 teaspoon salt
freshly ground black pepper to taste
1 teaspoon dried tarragon
2 tablespoons butter or margarine
2 tablespoons olive or vegetable oil
2 cups peeled diced tomatoes
2 medium onions, sliced, separated in rings
1 green pepper, cut in strips
1-1/2 cups chicken broth
1/2 cup white wine OR
additional chicken broth
1/4 cup tomato paste*

Make macaroni and set aside. Sprinkle chicken
with lemon juice, salt, pepper and tarragon.
Brown chicken in skillet with butter and oil. Add
tomatoes, onion rings, green pepper strips, 1/2
cup chicken broth, wine and tomato paste. Cover
and bring to a boil over high heat. Reduce heat
and simmer about 45 minutes until chicken is tender. Remove chicken and keep warm. Add
remaining 1 cup broth to the vegetables and bring
to a boil. Add in macaroni and continue to cook,
stirring occasionally, until macaroni is cooked al
dente. Place chicken in center of a warm platter.
Arrange macaroni around chicken. Serve immediately.

CHICKEN PASTA TOSS

1 full load of pasta dough made into shells
1 ounce butter or margarine
1 onion, finely chopped
1 clove garlic, crushed
2 cups cooked chicken, shredded
2 cups chicken stock
1/4 pound spinach leaves, shredded
freshly ground black pepper
1/4 cup pine nuts, toasted

Make shells, cook al dente, drain and remove to a heated serving platter. Melt butter in a large frying pan and cook onion and garlic, stirring, over a medium heat for 3 to 4 minutes. Add chicken and stock, and cook for 4-5 minutes longer. Add spinach to pan and season to taste with black pepper. Toss with pasta. Sprinkle with pine nuts and serve immediately.

Chapter 12

Each recipe serves 4 to 6 people
unless otherwise indicated.

————————————

Most of the recipes in this book
call for a full load of fresh pasta dough
made into a specific pasta shape using
the Automatic Pasta Maker.

————————————

All of the pasta dough recipes can be
mixed and rolled by hand and many of
the shapes can be cut by hand if you
don't have a machine.

————————————

You may substitute
16 ounces of dried pasta
for a full load of fresh pasta.

VEAL AND BROCCOLI LASAGNE

*1 full load of spinach pasta dough
made into lasagne
1 pound ground veal
1/4 cup chopped onion
2 cloves garlic, minced
2 tablespoons olive oil
1/4 pound mushrooms, chopped
1/2 green bell pepper, chopped
2 (6-ounce) cans tomato paste
1 teaspoon dried tarragon
2 tablespoons fresh basil, minced or
1 teaspoon dried basil
1/4 teaspoon dried oregano
1/2 teaspoon salt
1/4 teaspoon freshly ground black pepper
3 cups of water
1 cup thinly sliced broccoli florets
1-1/2 pounds cottage cheese
1-1/2 pounds mozzarella cheese, shredded
1/2 cup freshly grated Parmesan cheese*

Make lasagne, cook al dente, drain, and rinse. In large saucepan, brown veal over medium heat and drain. Set aside. In same pan, sauté onion and garlic in oil until transparent. Add veal, mushrooms and green pepper. Cook for 5 minutes. Stir in tomato paste, spices, and water. Simmer for 10-15 minutes. Spread 1/4 cup of sauce on bottom of 9 x 13-inch pan. Layer the following ingredients at least twice: lasagne noodles, sauce, broccoli, cottage cheese, mozzarella and Parmesan. Top with remaining sauce. Cover with greased foil. Bake at 375°F. for 1 hour.

ROTINI WITH EGGPLANT
AND BEEF SAUCE

1 full load of pasta dough made into rotini
1/2 pound ground sirloin
2 tablespoons olive oil
1/4 cup chopped onion
1/2 cup red bell pepper, diced
1 medium eggplant, peeled and cut into
1/2-inch cubes
1/3 cup beef broth, preferably unsalted
1 cup tomato, coarsely chopped
1 clove garlic, crushed through a press
salt to taste
freshly ground black pepper to taste
1 tablespoon freshly grated Parmesan cheese

Make rotini and set aside. Cook the ground beef in a large non-stick skillet over medium-high heat, crumbling the meat with the side of a spoon until browned, about 10 minutes. Transfer the browned ground beef to a strainer to drain off the fat. Wipe out the skillet, add the olive oil and heat over medium heat. Add the onion and bell pepper; stir to coat with the oil. Add the eggplant, raise the heat to high and cook, stirring often, 5 minutes. Add the beef broth and cook, stirring often, until the broth is absorbed, about 5 minutes. Add the cooked ground beef, chopped tomato and garlic. Cover, reduce the heat to medium and cook until the eggplant is tender, about 10 minutes. Uncover and cook until some of the liquid is evaporated and the sauce is slightly thickened, about 3 minutes. Season with the salt and pepper. Meanwhile, cook the rotini until al dente, drain, and transfer to a large heated serving bowl. Top with the sauce and toss. Sprinkle the Parmesan cheese over the top and serve.

PENNE WITH MINT SAUCE

1 full load of pasta dough made into penne
1 pound sweet Italian sausage, casings removed
2 large cloves garlic, minced
2 cups fresh mint, chopped
1 (16 ounce) can peeled tomatoes
coarsely chopped
1 cup water
1 teaspoon salt
freshly grated Parmesan cheese

Make penne and set aside. In large skillet, cook sausage, garlic and mint over medium-high heat until sausage is brown. Drain off grease. Transfer mixture to blender or food processor and process for 15 seconds or until sausage is coarsely chopped. Do not over process. Return mixture to skillet. Stir in tomatoes, water and salt. Cook over medium heat for 1 to 1-1/2 hours, or until sauce thickens. Meanwhile cook penne until al dente, drain, and transfer to a heated serving platter. Spoon sauce on top. Serve with freshly grated Parmesan cheese.

PAPPARDELLE WITH LAMB

1 full load of pasta dough made into pappardelle
1/2 cup olive oil
4 pounds boneless lamb
4 onions, sliced
1 teaspoon cayenne pepper
1 teaspoon ground tumeric
3 tablespoons ground cinnamon
1 teaspoon ground cloves
1/2 teaspoon saffron
5 carrots, sliced
2 peeled turnips, cubed
8 tomatoes, chopped
1 cup cooked chickpeas
1 cup cooked fava beans
2 zucchinis, cubed
1 green cabbage, sliced
1 cup raisins

Make papparadelle and set aside. Trim excess fat from lamb and cut into one-inch cubes. In a Dutch oven, cook the lamb and the onions in the olive oil until the meat begins to brown. Add the spices and enough water to cover the meat. Bring to a boil, then reduce the heat, cover the pot and let simmer for 45 minutes. When the meat has cooked for 45 minutes, add the rest of the ingredients and simmer until vegetables are tender. Meanwhile, cook the pappardelle, drain, and transfer to a heated serving platter. To serve, top the pasta with the lamb sauce and serve immediately.

VERMICELLI CARUSO

1 full load of pasta dough made into vermicelli
7 tablespoons olive oil, divided
1-1/2 cups onions, finely chopped
2 teaspoons garlic, finely chopped
2 (28 ounce) cans whole tomatoes
4 tablespoons tomato paste
1/2 teaspoon basil
1/4 teaspoon oregano
1/2 teaspoon sugar
3 teaspoons salt, divided
1 pound chicken livers
freshly ground black pepper to taste
flour

Make vermicelli and set aside. In a heavy skillet, heat 4 tablespoons oil over medium heat. Add onions and garlic. Cook, stirring until onions are soft and translucent. Stir in tomatoes and their liquid, tomato paste, basil, oregano, sugar, and 2 teaspoons salt. Bring mixture to a boil, then reduce heat. Simmer, loosely covered, for 30 minutes or longer, stirring occasionally. While sauce is cooking, sprinkle livers with pepper and 1 teaspoon salt. Dredge in flour. Heat remaining oil in heavy skillet. Brown livers over high heat; set aside. Meanwhile cook vermicelli until al dente, drain, and transfer to a heated serving bowl. Add chicken livers to sauce and reheat. Toss sauce with vermicelli and serve immediately.

SENSATIONAL LINGUINI

1 full load of pasta dough made into linguini
1 medium onion, diced
2 cloves garlic, minced
1/4 cup butter or margarine
1 tablespoon olive oil
1/2 pound ground sirloin
1/2 pound lean ground pork
1/2 pound ground veal
1/2 green bell pepper, chopped
1/2 pound mushrooms, chopped
2 (6-ounce) cans tomato paste
1 (28-ounce) can stewed Italian tomatoes
1-1/2 teaspoons Worcestershire sauce
1-1/2 teaspoons angostura bitters
1 tablespoon sugar
1/2 cup dry red wine
salt and freshly ground black pepper to taste
1/2 teaspoon celery salt
2 bay leaves
dash of cayenne pepper
freshly grated Parmesan cheese

In large, heavy kettle, sauté onion and garlic in butter and oil until transparent. Add beef, pork and veal, and brown over medium heat. Add green pepper, mushrooms, tomato paste, tomatoes, Worcestershire, bitters, sugar, wine, salt, pepper, celery salt, bay leaves and cayenne pepper. Simmer over low heat for 3 hours. Make linguini, cook until al dente, drain and transfer to warmed individual plates and top with sauce. Sprinkle with Parmesan to taste.

VEAL ITALIANO

1 full load of pasta dough made into spaghetti
1/2 cup all-purpose flour
1/2 teaspoon salt
1/2 teaspoon black pepper
1-1/2 pounds veal chunks
1/4 cup olive oil
2 garlic cloves, chopped
1 large onion, chopped
3 green bell peppers, cut into large chunks
1 (10-1/2 ounce) can chicken broth
1 (28 ounce) can whole tomatoes, undrained
1/4 cup red wine
1/2 teaspoon dried oregano
1/2 teaspoon dried basil
1/8 teaspoon crushed red pepper
1 teaspoon sugar

Make spaghetti and set aside. In a shallow dish, combine the flour with the salt and black pepper. Dredge the veal chunks in the mixture. Heat the oil in a Dutch oven over medium heat. Add the coated veal and cook until light golden about 10 minutes, stirring occasionally. Add the garlic, onion, and green peppers and cook for 5 minutes more, stirring occasionally. Add the chicken broth, tomatoes with juice, red wine, oregano, basil, red pepper, and sugar, reduce the heat, and simmer for 10 minutes more, stirring occasionally. Meanwhile, cook spaghetti until al dente, drain, and transfer to a heated serving platter. Spoon the veal mixture over the spaghetti and serve immediately.

CHEESY MEATBALLS WITH SPAGHETTI

1 full load of pasta dough made into spaghetti

CHEESY MEATBALLS
1 pound ground sirloin
2 tablespoons fresh parsley, finely chopped
1/2 cup Parmesan cheese, grated
2 teaspoons tomato paste
1 egg, beaten

TOMATO SAUCE
1/4 cup butter or margarine
1 onion, finely chopped
2 teaspoons dried basil
1 teaspoon dried oregano
1 (14 ounce) can of tomatoes,
undrained and mashed
2 tablespoons tomato paste (purée)
1/2 cup beef stock
1/2 cup white wine
1 teaspoon sugar
freshly ground black pepper to taste

Make spaghetti and set aside. To make meatballs, place beef, parsley, Parmesan cheese, tomato paste and egg in a bowl, and mix to combine. Form mixture into small balls and cook in a non-stick frying pan for 4-5 minutes or until brown. Remove meatballs from pan and drain on paper towel. To make sauce, melt butter in a large frying pan and cook onion, basil and oregano for 2-3 minutes or until onion is soft. Stir in tomatoes, tomato paste, beef

stock, wine and sugar. Bring to a boil, then reduce heat and simmer, stirring occasionally, for 30 minutes or until sauce reduces and thickens. Season to taste with black pepper. Add meatballs to sauce and cook for 5 minutes longer. Cook spaghetti until al dente, drain, and transfer to a heated serving platter. Top with meatballs and sauce. Serve immediately.

Prosciutto Delight

1 full load of pasta dough made into penne
1/4 cup unsalted butter
1/4 cup minced green onions
1/4 pound mushrooms, sliced
1/2 pound prosciutto, cut into 1/4-inch
julienne strips
1-1/2 cups heavy cream
1/2 teaspoon freshly ground black pepper
3/4 cup freshly grated Parmesan cheese

Make penne and set aside. In large skillet, melt butter and sauté onions, mushrooms and prosciutto for 3-5 minutes. Stir in cream and pepper. Heat to boiling then lower heat and simmer for 6-8 minutes or until sauce thickens slightly. Remove from heat. Meanwhile, cook penne until al dente, drain and transfer to a heated serving dish. Toss warm pasta with Parmesan. Pour prosciutto mixture over pasta and toss until evenly mixed. Serve immediately, sprinkled with additional Parmesan.

NEW YORK PASTA SPECIAL

1 full load of pasta dough made into fettuccini
1/2 pound sweet Italian sausage,
casings removed
1/2 pound hot Italian sausage, casings
removed
1/2 cup olive oil
1/2 cup butter
12 large mushrooms, sliced
2 cloves garlic, minced
1 large green bell pepper, chopped
1 cup green onions, chopped
1/4 cup minced fresh parsley
1/4 cup minced fresh basil or
2 teaspoons dried basil
2/3 cup freshly grated Parmesan cheese
1 cup sour cream

Make fettuccini and set aside. In large skillet, cook sausages over medium-high heat until brown. Remove sausage and set aside. Drain grease. Add olive oil and butter to skillet and sauté mushrooms, garlic, green pepper, green onions, parsley and basil until tender. Stir in sausage. Cook fettuccini until al dente, drain and transfer to a heated serving dish. Add sausage mixture, Parmesan and sour cream. Toss gently and serve immediately.

GOLDMINE LASAGNE

SAUCE
1 cup chopped onion
2 cloves garlic, crushed
1 (28 ounce) can crushed tomatoes
1 (16 ounce) can crushed tomatoes
1 (6 ounce) can tomato paste
1/4 cup minced fresh parsley
1 tablespoon packed light brown sugar
1 teaspoon salt
1-1/2 teaspoons dried oregano
1/4 teaspoon dried thyme
1 bay leaf
1 whole stalk celery, leaves removed
2 cups water

1 full load of pasta dough made into lasagne
1-1/2 to 2 pounds Italian sausage in casings
1 cup water
1 pound ricotta cheese
1-1/2 pounds mozzarella cheese, sliced

In large saucepan, combine all sauce ingredients and simmer for 3 hours, stirring occasionally. Remove bay leaf and celery stalk. In large skillet, cook sausage in water over medium heat. Cook until water evaporates. Cook under low heat and brown sausage about 5 minutes. Cut into 1/2-inch pieces. Add sausage to sauce. Cook lasagne, drain and rinse. In a 9 x 13-inch pan, layer half of noodles, sauce, ricotta and mozzarella. Repeat layers again. Cover with greased foil. Bake at 350°F. for 1 hour.

MARKET-STYLE SPAGHETTI

1 full load of pasta dough made into spaghetti
1 recipe marinara sauce (see recipe page 46)
6 black Sicilian olives, pitted
10 green olives, pitted
1 tablespoon pickled capers
3 tablespoons olive oil
1 clove garlic, finely sliced
1 small dried red chili pepper (or to taste),
broken into small pieces
1 teaspoon dried oregano
3/4 cup dry white wine

While the marinara sauce is cooking, chop the black olives, green olives and capers very fine. Also make spaghetti and set aside. In a small skillet, heat the oil over a medium flame and brown the garlic and chili pepper, about 1 minute. Add the olives, capers and oregano. Cook for 5 more minutes. Add the wine. Cover and let simmer for a few minutes. At this point, remove the garlic and chili pepper, then add the mixture to the marinara sauce. Let simmer for 5 more minutes. Meanwhile, cook spaghetti until al dente, drain, and transfer to a heated serving bowl. Add the sauce and toss until well mixed. Serve immediately.

SPAGHETTI ALLA CARBONARA

2 eggs
pinch of salt
1 tablespoon freshly grated Parmesan cheese
2 tablespoons olive oil
2 green onions, finely chopped
3/4 pound lean bacon, diced
1 tablespoon salt
1 tablespoon sweet butter
1/4 pound Parmesan cheese, freshly grated
2 tablespoons coarsely ground black pepper

Make spaghetti and set aside. In a small bowl, beat the egg with a pinch of salt and the 1 tablespoon cheese. Let stand. In a small skillet, heat the oil and lightly brown the scallions. Add the bacon and sauté well done, but not too crisp. Turn off the flame and let stand. Cook spaghetti until almost al dente (you will be reheating it in a few minutes when you blend in the other ingredients). Drain well. Place the butter in the spaghetti pot over a low flame and return the spaghetti to the pot. Mix in the bacon and green onions and stir well with a wooden fork. Add eggs. Keep tossing constantly over a low flame while adding the 1/4 pound cheese and the pepper. Within a couple of minutes, at the first sign of the eggs cooking, the pasta will be done. Serve from the pot into warmed pasta bowls.

ROTINI BAKED PORK CHOPS

1 half load of pasta dough made into short rotini
1 egg
2 tablespoons butter or margarine
6 rib or loin pork chops (2 to 2-1/2 pounds total)
about 3/4-inch thick
1 cup each finely chopped celery and onion
1 clove garlic, minced or pressed
1 medium-size carrot, coarsely shredded
1/4 cup chopped parsley
3/4 teaspoon salt
1/2 teaspoon each pepper, dry sage leaves, and
dry thyme leaves

Make rotini, cut into 1/4-inch lengths, cook until al dente, drain and rinse. Beat egg, stir in rotini to evenly coat and set aside. Melt butter in a wide frying pan over medium high heat. Add pork chops and cook, turning once, just until browned on both sides about 4 minutes total. Remove chops from pan and set aside. Reduce heat to medium and add celery, onion, garlic, and carrot. Cook, stirring often, until vegetables are soft but not brown for about 6 to 8 minutes. Remove from heat and stir in parsley, salt, pepper, sage, and thyme. Then lightly stir vegetable mixture into pasta mixture. Place a pork chop at one end of a greased 7 x 11-inch baking dish. Spoon about a fifth of the pasta mixture over chop. Place another chop over pasta, overlapping it slightly. Continue alternating pasta and chops. Spoon any remaining pasta mixture around chops. Cover and bake in a 350°F. oven 25 to 30 minutes.

POLISH SAUSAGE, ZUCCHINI & RIGATONI

1 full load of pasta dough made into rigatoni
***OR** small macaroni*
4 tablespoons red wine vinegar
2 tablespoons Dijon-style mustard
1 tablespoon dry basil
1 pound Polish sausage (kielbasa),
cut into 1/4-inch-thick slices
1 medium-size red onion, thinly sliced
4 small zucchini, thinly sliced
1 bunch watercress (about 6 ounces),
washed and crisped

Make rigatoni, cook until al dente, drain well, and set aside. While pasta is cooking, in a small bowl, stir together vinegar, mustard, and basil; set aside. Cook sausage slices in a large frying pan over medium-high heat stirring frequently. Add onion and stir until softened. Add cooked pasta and vinegar mixture; stir until heated through about 2 minutes. Stir in zucchini and cook just until tender-crisp about 3 minutes. Transfer to a heated serving platter, garnish with a bouquet of watercress and serve at once.

SHELLS WITH LAMB

1 full load of pasta dough made into shells
1 (2-pound) leg of lamb, cut in serving pieces
juice of 1 lemon (about 2 tablespoons)
1-1/2 teaspoons salt
freshly ground black pepper to taste
1/4 cup olive oil
2 tablespoons all-purpose flour
1 (6 ounce) can tomato paste
4 cups hot water
1 medium onion
10 whole cloves
2 (2-inch) cinnamon sticks, broken
2 garlic cloves, cut in half
1 orange
1/3 cup grated Parmesan cheese
1 lemon slice for garnish

Sprinkle lamb pieces with lemon juice, salt and pepper. Heat oil in large heavy pot or Dutch oven. Brown lamb pieces slowly on all sides, about 20 minutes. Remove lamb pieces; set aside. Stir flour into drippings. Continue stirring until lightly browned. Mix tomato paste and hot water. Stir into flour mixture. Add browned lamb pieces. Stud onion with cloves. Punch holes in the onion with a metal skewer and the cloves will slide into the onion easier.

Place onion, cinnamon sticks and garlic on a 5-inch square piece of cheesecloth. Bring edges together and tie with string to make a spice bag. Place bag in sauce. Cut orange in half. Squeeze orange juice into sauce. Add orange halves to sauce and bring to a boil. Cover and reduce heat. Simmer 1 hour until lamb is tender. Remove and discard spice bag and orange halves. Remove lamb and keep warm. Bring sauce to a boil and add shells. Bring to a boil again. Cook 2 to 3 minutes stirring occasionally to keep shells from sticking. Continue cooking until shells are al dente. Transfer pasta and sauce to a heated serving platter. Sprinkle with Parmesan cheese. Toss lightly. Arrange lamb pieces on the platter with shells then garnish with lemon slices.

VARIATION: Try substituting 2 pounds cubed beef sirloin for lamb and macaroni in place of shells.

FUSILLI WITH SAUSAGE AND CREAM SAUCE

1 full load of pasta dough made into fusilli
1/4 cup butter
1-1/2 pounds sweet Italian sausage,
casings removed
2 cups heavy cream
1 cup dry white wine
1 tablespoon minced fresh parsley
1/2 teaspoon nutmeg
1 cup freshly grated Parmesan cheese
1 tablespoon minced fresh parsley

Make fusilli and set aside. In large skillet, melt butter. Stir in sausage and fry until brown. Remove sausage and drain grease. Return sausage to skillet

and stir in cream, wine, 1 tablespoon parsley, nutmeg and 1/2 cup Parmesan cheese. Simmer for 3-4 minutes. Cook fusilli until al dente, drain, and transfer to a heated serving platter. Stir in 2 tablespoons of sausage mixture and remaining 1/2 cup Parmesan cheese. Toss until pasta is coated. Pour remaining sausage mixture over pasta. Sprinkle with 1 tablespoon parsley and serve immediately.

International Favorites

Chapter 13

Each recipe serves 4 to 6 people
unless otherwise indicated.

———————

Most of the recipes in this book
call for a full load of fresh pasta dough
made into a specific pasta shape using
the Automatic Pasta Maker.

———————

All of the pasta dough recipes can be
mixed and rolled by hand and many of
the shapes can be cut by hand if you
don't have a machine.

———————

You may substitute
16 ounces of dried pasta
for a full load of fresh pasta.

Cold Japanese-Style Noodles

Salad
*1 full load of buckwheat pasta dough (use soba
variation) made into oriental noodles
1 daikon (Oriental radish), peeled and grated
into thin shreds
1 carrot, peeled and grated into thin shreds
1 cucumber, peeled, seeded and cut
into thin strips
3 green onions, trimmed and chopped
2 tablespoons rice-wine vinegar
1 tablespoon mirin or sweet sherry
1/2 teaspoon each sugar and salt*

Sweet & Sour Japanese Dressing
*1/4 cup defatted chicken stock
6 tablespoons reduced-sodium soy sauce
6 tablespoons mirin (sweet Japanese rice wine)
2 teaspoons peeled, grated fresh ginger
2 green onions, trimmed and finely chopped
1 tablespoon sesame seeds, toasted, for garnish*

Make *soba* oriental noodles and cook al dente.
Drain and rinse thoroughly to cool. Combine vegetables in bowl. Add vinegar, mirin, sugar and salt.
Mix well and refrigerate. To prepare dressing,
combine all ingredients and mix well. To serve,
arrange noodles on large platter. Arrange vegetables on top. Garnish with sesame seeds. Pass
dressing at table. The salad should be served in
bowls rather than on plates. The amount of dressing may seem excessive, but the salad is best with
lots of dressing. Encourage your guests to be gen-

erous with the dressing let them know that it's an accepted Japanese custom to drink up the extra in their bowls once the noodles have been eaten. If you have the time, make the salad early in the day and serve it icy cold. (Salad can be held for up to 12 hours by refrigerating noodles, vegetables and dressing in separate airtight containers.) A more authentic Japanese recipe would call for dashi, a stock made from dried bonito shavings and kornbu, a type of kelp, in the dressing. But for convenience, chicken stock is used in its place.

MEDITERRANEAN PASTA SALAD

1 full load of pasta dough made into shells
3/4 pound fresh spinach, rinsed and
coarsely chopped
1/2 pound feta cheese, crumbled
1/2 cup Italian dressing
1/2 cup vegetable oil
1 tablespoon chopped fresh basil or
1-1/2 teaspoons dried basil
1 tablespoon grated Parmesan cheese
1 tablespoon wine vinegar
salt and freshly ground black pepper to taste

Make shells and cook until al dente. Then drain, rinse thoroughly in cold water and set aside to cool. Meanwhile, in a large bowl, mix together all the remaining ingredients thoroughly but gently. Add the pasta and toss. Serve or refrigerate until ready to serve but salad is best when served at room temperature.

TROPICAL CHICKEN PASTA SALAD

SALAD
1 full load of pasta dough made into rotini
***OR** shells*
juice of 1 lime (3 tablespoons)
1 tablespoon peanut oil
1 tablespoon soy sauce
1 large clove garlic
peeled ginger (1-inch piece)
1/2 pound boneless, skinless chicken breast
1 green bell pepper, finely diced
1 carrot, trimmed, peeled and grated
1 (16 ounce) can crushed pineapple
in unsweetened pineapple juice, drained,
with 1/4 cup liquid reserved

CILANTRO-MAYONNAISE DRESSING
1/4 cup juice from canned pineapple
juice of 2 limes (6 tablespoons)
1/2 cup mayonnaise
1 tablespoon peanut oil
1/2 cup chopped fresh cilantro
Salt and fleshly ground black pepper to taste

Preheat grill or broiler. Make rotini and cook until al dente. Drain and rinse thoroughly to cool. Transfer to large mixing bowl. In blender, combine lime juice, peanut oil, soy sauce, garlic and ginger. Blend until smooth. Pour over chicken breasts. Grill or broil for 6 to 8 minutes per side, basting once or twice with marinade, until meat feels firm and looks white throughout. Remove from grill and dice. Add chicken, green pepper, carrot and pineapple to pasta. Toss. To prepare dressing: Combine reserved pineapple juice, lime juice, mayonnaise, oil and cilantro in blender and blend until creamy smooth. Pour dressing over salad. Season to taste with salt and pepper. Serve at once or hold in refrigerator for a few hours. Leftovers can be refreshed with additional lime or pineapple juice.

CREOLE NOODLES

1 full load of pasta dough made into fettuccine
3/4 pound cooked ham in one piece
2 medium-size celery stalks, sliced
1 small onion, diced
1 tablespoon salad oil
2 (14-1/2 ounce) cans stewed tomatoes
1 (10 ounce) package frozen whole-kernel corn
1 (10 ounce) package frozen whole okra
1 tablespoon creole seasoning
celery leaves for garnish

Make fettuccine, cook until al dente, drain and transfer to a heated serving platter. Cut ham into 3/4-inch chunks. Meanwhile, heat salad oil in a 4-quart saucepan and cook celery and onion, stirring occasionally, for about 5 minutes. Stir in ham and continue cooking until ham is lightly browned. Add tomatoes, corn, okra, and creole seasoning and bring to a boil. Reduce heat to low, cover and simmer about 10 minutes until vegetables are tender. To serve, spoon mixture over pasta and toss gently. Garnish with celery leaves.

CHINESE BARBECUED PORK AND NOODLE SALAD

PORK
2 tablespoons soy sauce
2 tablespoons sherry
1 tablespoon hoisin sauce
3/4 pound boneless pork tenderloin

SALAD AND MARINADE
1 full load of Chinese egg noodle dough made into oriental noodles or vermicelli
1 tablespoon sesame oil
3 tablespoons hoisin sauce
3 tablespoons reduced-sodium soy sauce
2 tablespoons rice-wine vinegar
1 teaspoon sugar
1 cup fresh snow peas, trimmed
1 cup bean sprouts
3 large stalks bok choy
6 green onions, trimmed, slivered lengthwise and cut into 2-inch pieces

Make marinade for pork by combining marinade ingredients in a shallow bowl large enough to hold pork. Add pork and roll in marinade to coat. (Pork can be marinated for up to 8 hours if desired, but it is not necessary.) Be sure to refrigerate if marinating for more than 30 minutes. When you are ready to make salad, preheat grill. Make oriental noodles and cook al dente. Drain and rinse thoroughly to cool. Place in large bowl and toss with sesame oil. In small bowl, mix hoisin sauce, soy sauce, rice-wine vinegar and

sugar. Add to the pasta and toss. While pasta cooks, briefly blanch snow peas, bean sprouts and bok choy in boiling water to cover for 45 seconds. Immediately plunge into ice water to stop cooking, then drain. The vegetables should be blanched briefly to set the color and to cook out the slightly bitter flavor of the raw bean sprouts. Chinese barbecue sauce, known as hoisin, is the main flavoring agent of this warm salad. It is available in most supermarkets, as are bok choy (a vegetable that resembles a cross between celery and cabbage) and snow peas. Cook pork on a hot grill for 3 to 10 minutes per side, depending on thickness. Pork is done when meat is firm throughout and just barely shows pink. Do not overcook. Cut into matchstick-size pieces. Add vegetables and pork to noodles. Toss to mix well. Serve at once.

SPANISH PASTA WITH SHELLFISH

1 full load of pasta dough made into spaghetti
cut into 3-inch lengths
1/2 cup olive oil, or more as needed for sautéing
1 pound shrimp, shelled and deveined
1 pound cleaned squid, sliced into rings, tentacles
separated
1/2 cup chopped shallots OR red onion
2 tablespoons minced or pressed garlic
1 cup peeled, seeded, and chopped
fresh or drained canned tomato
3 quarts chicken stock
1 teaspoon crumbled saffron threads

salt and ground cayenne pepper to taste
1/2 cup sliced pitted flavorful green olives
*About 24 mussels **OR** clams, **OR** a*
combination of both
roasted red sweet pepper, cut into
strips, for garnish
fresh herb sprigs such as marjoram
***OR** flat-leaf parsley for garnish*
lemon wedges for squeezing

Make spaghetti, cook until al dente, drain, rinse and set aside. In a paella pan or large sauté pan, heat the oil over medium-high heat. Add the shrimp and sauté until they turn bright pink. Remove shrimp with a slotted utensil and set aside. Add the squid and sauté until opaque, about 1 minute. Remove squid with a slotted utensil and set aside. Add the shallots or onion to the pan and sauté about 3 minutes. Add the spaghetti and sauté until golden, about 5 minutes. Add the garlic and tomato and sauté about 1 minute longer. Stir in the chicken stock, saffron, and salt and cayenne to taste and bring to a boil. Cook, stirring almost continuously, until the pasta is almost tender and only a little liquid remains, about 20 minutes. Stir the olives into the pasta, then arrange the mussels or clams and the shrimp and squid over the pasta. Reduce the heat to low, cover, and cook until the liquid is absorbed and the pasta begins to crust around the edges, 6 to 8 minutes. Remove from the heat and let stand about 5 minutes before serving. Garnish with sweet pepper strips and herb sprigs. Offer lemon wedges to squeeze over the top at the table.

THAI CHICKEN & PASTA

1 full load of pasta dough made into linguine
2 large green onions
1 large.carrot
1 small zucchini
1-1/2 pounds skinless, boneless chicken thighs
1 tablespoon vegetable oil
1 tablespoon minced peeled gingerroot
1/3 cup soy sauce
1/3 cup creamy peanut butter
3 tablespoons chili sauce
3 tablespoons seasoned rice vinegar
1/4 teaspoon coconut extract
peanuts for garnish

Make fettuccini and set aside. Thinly slice green onions and cut carrot and zucchini into pencil-thin strips. Cut each chicken thigh into 6 pieces. In nonstick 12-inch skillet over medium-high heat, cook half the chicken thighs at a time until golden brown. With slotted spoon, remove chicken thighs to plate as they brown. Add the vegetable oil to the same skillet and cook gingerroot and carrots until carrots are lightly browned. Stir in zucchini and green onions and continue cooking until vegetables are tender. Remove vegetable mixture to small bowl and keep warm. Into the same skillet, now stir in soy sauce, peanut butter, chili sauce, rice vinegar, coconut extract, and 1-1/4 cups water until well blended. Return chicken thighs to skillet with peanut sauce and bring to a boil. Reduce heat to low; cover and simmer until chicken loses its pink color throughout, about 5 minutes. Meanwhile cook fettuccini until al dente, drain and transfer to a heated serving bowl. Top with chicken mixture and toss. Spoon carrot mixture over chicken and garnish with peanuts.

ORIENTAL NOODLES AND VEGETABLES

1 full load of udon pasta dough
made into fettuccini
1 tablespoon peanut oil
2 teaspoons grated fresh ginger
1 clove garlic, crushed
1 onion, sliced
1 carrot, sliced diagonally
3 stalks celery or bok choy, sliced diagonally
2 cups bean sprouts
1/2 pound snow peas, trimmed
freshly ground black pepper

Make fettuccini and cook until almost al dente. Drain and set aside. Heat oil in a wok or a large frying pan and stir-fry ginger and garlic for 1 to 2 minutes. Add onion and carrot and stir-fry for 4 to 5 minutes longer. Toss in celery, bean sprouts and snow peas and cook for another 2 to 3 minutes. Stir in noodles and cook for 3 to 4 minutes or until noodles are heated. Season to taste with black pepper and serve immediately.

AFGHANISTAN-STYLE LEEK-STUFFED RAVIOLI WITH YOGURT AND MEAT SAUCES

1 full load of pasta dough made into ravioli
1 egg
1/2 recipe Bolognese Meat Sauce (see page 45)
2 teaspoons ground cinnamon
1-1/2 teaspoons ground cumin
3 tablespoons olive oil
1-1/2 cups chopped leek, including green portion
salt and freshly ground black pepper to taste
2 cups plain yogurt
1 teaspoon minced or pressed garlic
1/4 cup minced fresh mint
3 tablespoons unsalted butter, melted
julienned leek, green portion only, for garnish
fresh mint leaves **OR** *oregano for garnish*

Prepare the Bolognese meat sauce according to the recipe and add the cinnamon and cumin to the sauce while it simmers. In a sauté pan or skillet, heat the oil over medium heat. Add the chopped leek and sauté until very tender, about 10 minutes. Season to taste with salt and pepper. Remove from the heat and set aside. In a bowl, combine the yogurt, garlic, and 1/4 cup mint. Salt to taste and set aside. Make ravioli according to instructions for making filled pasta in the Making Pasta chapter. You can assemble ravioli as directed using the Ravioli Cutter for smaller shapes to make about 50 ravioli or by hand method to make larger shapes. After spooning on filling, be sure to brush the exposed bottom layer of dough with beaten egg before covering with the top layer of dough. Pinch the edges of the dough together to seal making sure to force out the air. Cook the ravioli until al dente. Do this in batches if necessary, then drain the pasta and toss with the melted butter. To serve, spoon a portion of the minted yogurt onto each plate. Top with ravioli and a dollop of the meat sauce over the top. Garnish with leek greens and mint leaves or oregano and serve immediately.

VARIATION: Please note that you can substitute Won Ton or Chinese Egg Noodle pasta dough when making this recipe.

GREEK PASTA SALAD

1 full load of pasta dough made into rotini OR
short fusilli
1/2 cup finely chopped red onion
1 cup ripe olives, chopped
2 cups crumbled feta cheese
1/4 cup finely chopped green bell pepper
2 small tomatoes, chopped
3/4 cup olive or vegetable oil
6 tablespoons red wine vinegar
1-1/2 teaspoons salt
1/2 teaspoon black pepper
1 teaspoon sugar
2 teaspoons Dijon-style mustard

Make rotini and cook until al dente. Then drain, rinse thoroughly in cold water and set aside to cool. When pasta has cooled slightly add the onion, olives, feta cheese, green pepper, and tomatoes. In a small bowl, whisk together the remaining ingredients to make dressing. Pour dressing over the pasta and toss gently. Refrigerate until ready to serve.

ITALIAN PASTA PIE

*1 half load of pasta dough made into
rotini OR macaroni
1 cup bottled marinara OR spaghetti sauce
2 cups mozzarella cheese, shredded
2 cups all-purpose flour
salt
3/4 cup shortening or margarine
1 large egg
1 pound part-skim ricotta cheese
1 (7-ounce) package refrigerated pesto sauce
freshly ground black pepper to taste
1 tablespoon freshly grated Parmesan cheese*

Make rotini and cook until al dente. Drain and return to pot. Stir in marinara sauce and 1 cup shredded mozzarella and set aside. Meanwhile, in large bowl, combine flour and 1/2 teaspoon salt. With pastry blender, cut in shortening until mixture resembles coarse crumbs. With fork, stir in 4 to 5 tablespoons cold water just until mixture holds together. Shape dough into a ball and set aside. In cup, lightly beat egg and reserve 1 tablespoon beaten egg for brushing on crust later. Place remaining egg in a medium bowl. Stir in ricotta cheese, pesto sauce, and pepper. On lightly floured surface, with floured rolling pin, roll two-thirds of dough into rectangle 2 inches larger all around than inverted 11 x 7-inch glass baking dish. Gently ease dough into baking dish, allowing dough to hang over edge. Sprinkle remaining 1 cup mozzarella cheese over bottom of dough in baking dish. Top with half of pesto mixture, all of

rotini mixture, then the remaining pesto mixture. Preheat oven to 400°F. Roll remaining dough into 12 x 8-inch rectangle and lift it onto top of pie. Fold overhang under and pinch to form stand-up edge. Flute with the tines of a fork. Cut slits in top of crust to allow steam to escape during baking. Brush top of pie with reserved egg and sprinkle with grated Parmesan cheese. Bake pie 40 to 45 minutes until crust is golden brown and filling is hot.

GOLDEN NOODLES WITH CHILE DIPPING SAUCE

CHILI DIPPING SAUCE
4 fresh red hot chilies, stemmed
2 garlic cloves, peeled
1/4 cup freshly squeezed lime juice
2 tablespoons soy sauce
2 tablespoons sesame oil

1 full load of Chinese Egg Noodle dough
made into vermicelli
2 tablespoons vegetable oil
salt and freshly ground black pepper to taste
ground cayenne pepper
1/2 cup finely chopped green onion,
including green tops
1/2 cup finely chopped bamboo shoots
OR water chestnuts
1/4 cup minced fresh cilantro
3 tablespoons minced fresh red hot chile

3 eggs, beaten
oil for deep-fat frying
toasted sesame seeds for topping
soy sauce for dipping

To make the dipping sauce, combine all ingredients in a food processor or blender and blend well. Set aside. Make vermicelli, cook until al dente, drain and transfer to a large mixing bowl. Toss the pasta with the 2 tablespoons vegetable oil and season to taste with salt and black and cayenne peppers. Stir in the green onions, bamboo shoots or water chestnuts, cilantro, and chile. Add the eggs and mix well. Pour the oil in a deep-fat fryer or deep saucepan to a depth of 2 inches and preheat to 360°F. Using your hands, gently form the noodle mixture into loose balls about the size of golf balls, or larger, if desired. Fry the balls, a few at a time, until golden brown, 3 to 4 minutes. The noodles will separate during cooking to form irregular shapes. Use a slotted utensil to help keep them intact as much as possible during frying. Drain balls on paper towel and sprinkle with sesame seeds.. This is a great appetizer and should be served hot with the chile sauce and soy sauce for dipping.

THAI FRIED NOODLES

1 full load of udon OR won ton pasta dough
made into vermicelli
6 tablespoons soy sauce
4 teaspoons rice wine vinegar OR
distilled white vinegar
2 tablespoons sugar
4 teaspoons paprika
1/2 cup vegetable oil, or more if needed
1/2 pound boneless pork OR boned and skinned
chicken breast, cut into very small pieces
2 tablespoons garlic, minced or pressed
2 teaspoons ground dried red hot chile, OR
1 tablespoon minced fresh hot chile
4 eggs, lightly beaten
1/2 pound medium-sized shrimp,
shelled and de-veined, tails left intact
1-1/2 cups fresh bean sprouts
3 green onions, including tops, thinly sliced
1/2 cup chopped unsalted dry-roasted peanuts
1/4 cup fresh cilantro, chopped
dried shrimp, finely minced, for garnish
fresh cilantro sprigs and lemon or lime wedges
for garnish

Make vermicelli and cut into 6-inch strips. Cook until al dente, drain, rinse and set aside. Toss gently after adding the noodles to avoid breaking them. In a small bowl, combine the soy sauce, vinegar, sugar, and paprika. Set aside. Because this is a stir-fry recipe, assemble all of the ingredients within arm's reach before heating the wok or frying pan. Heat a wok or frying pan over high heat. Add the oil and swirl to coat the pan. Add the pork or chicken, garlic, and chile and stir-fry for 1 minute. Stir in the drained noodles and the soy sauce mixture and stir-fry about 30 seconds. Push the noodles to one side, pour in about a tablespoon more oil, if necessary, and add the eggs; cook just until slightly set, then break them up. Add the shrimp and stir-fry just until they turn pink. Add most of the bean sprouts, the green onion, and 1/4 cup of the peanuts and stir-fry until the sprouts and onions are crisp-tender, 1 to 2 minutes. Remove from the heat and transfer to a serving plate. Sprinkle with the chopped cilantro, remaining 1/4 cup peanuts, and dried shrimp (if used). Garnish with the remaining bean sprouts, cilantro sprigs, and lemon or lime wedges, and serve immediately.

VARIATION: Soybean curd (tofu) may be added along with or substituted for the meat.

PAN-FRIED DUMPLINGS (POTSTICKERS)

12 ounces ground lean pork
1 cup finely chopped onion
1 cup finely chopped napa or
other Asian-type cabbage
1 tablespoon fresh ginger root, minced or grated
1 tablespoon Asian-style sesame oil
1 tablespoon soy sauce
salt and freshly ground black pepper to taste
1 full load of Buckwheat OR Won Ton pasta
dough, cut into 3-inch circles,
Peanut oil for pan frying
2 cups homemade chicken stock or
canned chicken broth
Chinese chives for garnish

Make won tons according to instructions for making filled pasta in the Making Pasta chapter. You'll need about 36 3-inch circles. Keep the dough covered to prevent it from drying out. In a bowl, combine the pork, onion, cabbage, ginger root, sesame oil, soy sauce, and salt and pepper to taste. Mix well and set aside. Spoon about 2 teaspoons of the pork mixture onto a dough circle and follow the instructions for making won ton in the Making Pasta chapter. To make a traditional potsticker you'll need to pinch the dough together at the top into 3 little pleats so that the dumpling resembles a little bag that has been squeezed shut. Heat a skillet over high heat. Add just enough peanut or other vegetable oil to cover the bottom, then swirl the pan to coat bottom and sides. Reduce heat to medium. Add the dumplings, smooth side down, so that they touch each other in straight rows or in a circle. Increase the heat so that the oil sizzles. Cook until the bottoms are browned, then pour in enough stock or broth to come halfway up the sides of the dumplings. Reduce the heat so that the liquid simmers, cover the pot, and cook until the liquid is almost absorbed. Uncover and cook until the bottoms of the dumplings are crisp, adding a bit more oil underneath the dumplings, if necessary. Remove from the heat and, using a spatula, transfer to a plate, and garnish with chives. Serve immediately with soy sauce, rice vinegar, Chinese black vinegar, or hot chile oil for dipping.

GREEK PASTA CASSEROLE

1 full load of pasta dough made into macaroni
olive or vegetable oil
1 large onion, chopped
3/4 pound ground sirloin
1 (28-ounce) can Italian plum tomatoes
1/2 teaspoon sugar
1/4 teaspoon ground cinnamon
3 tablespoons all purpose flour
1/8 teaspoon ground nutmeg
3-1/4 cups milk
2 large eggs
freshly grated Parmesan cheese
1/4 cup plain dried bread crumbs

Add one tablespoon of vegetable oil to a12-inch skillet over medium heat and cook onion until tender. Increase heat to medium-high. Add ground sirloin and cook, stirring occasionally, until all pan juices evaporate and meat is browned. Add tomatoes with their liquid, sugar, cinnamon, and 3/4 teaspoon salt, stirring to break up tomatoes. Bring to a boil. Reduce heat to low and simmer for 5 minutes. Meanwhile, cook macaroni until al dente, drain and return to pan. Preheat oven to 350°F. To prepare sauce, add 2 tablespoons of vegetable oil to a 3-quart saucepan over medium heat and stir in flour, nutmeg, and 1 teaspoon salt, until blended. Cook 1 minute. Gradually stir in milk and cook, stirring constantly, until mixture boils and thickens for about 10 minutes. Remove saucepan from heat. In small bowl, beat eggs slightly. Into eggs, beat small amount of the hot milk mixture. Slowly pour egg mixture back into milk mixture, stirring constantly until blended. Stir in meat mixture and 1/4 cup Parmesan into macaroni in pan. Spoon into deep 4-quart casserole. Carefully pour sauce over macaroni mixture. In small bowl, mix bread crumbs with 1/4 cup Parmesan cheese, then sprinkle over sauce. Bake, uncovered, 40 minutes or until hot and custard is set. Let stand 10 minutes for easier serving.

Desserts

Chapter 14

Each recipe serves 4 to 6 people
unless otherwise indicated.

———————

Most of the recipes in this book
call for a full load of fresh pasta dough
made into a specific pasta shape using
the Automatic Pasta Maker.

———————

All of the pasta dough recipes can be
mixed and rolled by hand and many of
the shapes can be cut by hand if you
don't have a machine.

———————

You may substitute
16 ounces of dried pasta
for a full load of fresh pasta.

CHOCOLATE & NUT BUTTERFLIES

1 half load of pasta dough made into butterflies
1/4 cup blanched almonds
1/4 cup hazelnuts
2 tablespoons butter or margarine
2 squares semi-sweet chocolate, coarsely chopped
2 tablespoons light-brown sugar

Make butterflies, cook al dente, drain and transfer to a heated serving dish. Meanwhile, put nuts in a broiler pan and broil, stirring frequently, until golden brown. Chop nuts coarsely. Add butter to pasta and stir. Add chopped nuts, chocolate and brown sugar. Toss to mix thoroughly. Serve at once.

ALMOND RAVIOLI WITH RASPBERRY SAUCE

1 half load of pasta dough made into ravioli
1-1/4 cups ground almonds
1/2 cup powdered sugar
2 egg yolks
2 tablespoons butter or margarine
plain yogurt
raspberry leaves, if desired

RASPBERRY SAUCE
4 cups raspberries
1/2 cup powdered sugar

In a bowl, mix together ground almonds, powdered sugar and egg yolks. In a small saucepan,

237

melt butter. Add to almond mixture. Make ravioli according to the instructions in the Making Pasta chapter filling them with the ground almond paste. Cook ravioli until al dente, drain, and set aside. To make sauce, mix raspberries and sugar in a medium-size saucepan (be sure to save a few raspberries for garnish). Heat gently until juice begins to run. Press through a sieve. To serve pour a pool of sauce on 4 dessert plates and arrange ravioli on top. Spoon a dollop of yogurt on top and decorate with reserved raspberries and raspberry leaves, if desired.

FRIED COFFEE-PASTA BOWLS

1 full load of pasta dough OR Coffee Pasta dough
made into linguine
vegetable oil for deep-fat frying
2 cups honey
1/4 cup cognac
1 cup chopped pistachios OR almonds
coffee or vanilla ice cream
fresh mint leaves for garnish

Make linguine, divide into 6 portions, and form each portion into a bowl. Meanwhile, pour the oil to a depth of 2 inches in a deep-fat fryer and preheat to about 365°F. Put the bowl into a wire strainer and carefully lower into the oil. Hold it in position until the pasta is crisp and lightly golden about 2 to 3 minutes. Transfer the nest, bottom side up, to paper towel to drain while frying the other nests. (This can be done 3 to 4 hours in advance of serving.) In a saucepan, combine the honey and cognac over low heat. Cook, stirring almost continuously, until the honey comes to a boil. Reduce the heat to low and simmer for about 2 minutes. Remove from the heat and cool to luke-warm. Just before serving, invert the nests and place them on plates. Sprinkle each nest with some of the nuts and spoon the honey mixture over the top to coat the nests. Add a scoop of ice cream in the center, sprinkle with the remaining nuts, garnish with mint or scented geranium, and serve immediately.

VARIATION: For a change make with chocolate pasta (recipe follows) and chocolate ice cream.

COFFEE & CHOCOLATE PASTA

2 pasta measuring cups of all-purpose flour
3 eggs, room temperature
1 teaspoon olive oil
1/4 teaspoon salt (optional)
1/4 cup espresso powder
1/2 cup of strongly-brewed coffee
1/2 cup powdered sugar

Blend all ingredients except the flour together thoroughly. Then slowly add to flour according to the directions in your Pasta Maker Instruction booklet.

VARIATION: For chocolate pasta substitute 1/2 cup powdered cocoa mixed with 1/2 cup water for espresso powder, coffee and powdered sugar.

BAVARIAN STRUDEL ROLLS

1 full load of Pasta All'uovo made into cannelloni
1 tablespoon butter or margarine, melted
3 cups hot milk
powdered sugar for garnish

APPLE FILLING
4 cups, finely sliced, peeled apples
1/2 cup sugar
2/3 cup finely chopped walnuts
1/2 cup coarse dry bread crumbs
1/2 cup golden raisins
1 teaspoon cinnamon
nutmeg to taste

Make cannelloni according to instructions for cutting pasta shapes in the Making Pasta chapter. You'll need about 18 sheets 4 x 6-inch. Cook the pieces of pasta, a few at a time if necessary, until al dente. Drain and rinse under cold water, then lay out on double-thick paper towels. Preheat the oven to 400° F. To make Apple Filling combine all ingredients in a large bowl and blend thoroughly. Spread filling onto pasta sheets leaving a 1/2-inch strip uncovered on one edge. Roll up jelly-roll fashion toward uncovered edge. Pinch with fingers along edge to seal. Place rolls in a 13x 9-inch buttered baking dish seam-side down. Brush tops with melted butter. Pour hot milk over strudel rolls. Bake until golden in preheated oven, 20 minutes. To serve, place strudel rolls into a dessert dish. Spoon some of the hot milk from the baking dish over the rolls and sprinkle with powdered sugar. For a change, try substituting 1 (21 ounce) can cherry pie filling for apples. Mix 2/3 cup chopped nuts and 1/2 cup raisins with pie filling. Garnish with powdered sugar.

RASPBERRY-MACADAMIA MANICOTTI

1 full load of pasta dough sweetened with 4 tablespoons of sugar made into manicotti

RASPBERRY SAUCE
2 cups fresh raspberries
1/2 cup water
1/2 cup sugar
2 tablespoons red currant jelly
2 tablespoons water
1 tablespoon cornstarch
2 tablespoons orange-flavored liqueur

MACADAMIA FILLING
14 ounces cream cheese, room temperature
1/2 cup finely chopped macadamia nuts

Make manicotti according to instructions for cutting pasta shapes in the Making Pasta chapter. You'll need about 16 sheets 5 x 6-inch. Cook the pieces of pasta, a few at a time if necessary, until al dente. Drain and rinse under cold water, then lay out on double-thick paper towels. Preheat the oven to 400° F. In a medium saucepan, mix raspberries with 1/2 cup water and sugar. Bring to a boil. Remove from heat and press through a sieve. Place in a

241

small saucepan. Set aside. In a small bowl, blend together currant jelly, 2 tablespoons water and cornstarch. Add to raspberry mixture. Bring to a boil. Cook and stir constantly over medium heat until thickened. Remove from heat. Set aside. To make Macadamia Filling combine cream cheese, nuts and liqueur in a small bowl. Spread about 2 heaping tablespoons of Macadamia Filling down the center of one side of each pasta sheet. Fold sides of pasta over filling to cover ends of tube and roll shut. Place seam side down on dessert plates and top with Raspberry Sauce. To serve flambé-style, place orange-flavored liqueur in a small saucepan over low heat to warm. Do not boil. Pour over Raspberry Sauce and ignite. Serve flaming.

CARAMELIZED APPLE-CINNAMON NOODLE PUDDING

1 half load of pasta dough made into macaroni
2 tablespoons butter or margarine
2 cups apples cut into 1/4 to 1/2-inch pieces
2 tablespoons light brown sugar
2 tablespoons golden raisins
1/4 teaspoon ground cinnamon
1 cup small curd creamed cottage cheese
1/2 cup sugar
3 eggs
2 cups milk, scalded
1 teaspoon vanilla extract
pinch of nutmeg

Make macaroni, cook until al dente, drain and set

aside. Heat butter in medium skillet and stir in the apples and sprinkle with brown sugar. Sauté, stirring, until apples are glazed and slightly caramelized. Stir in raisins and cinnamon. Beat the cottage cheese and the sugar until fairly smooth. Beat in the eggs, one at a time, beating well after each addition. Stir in the milk and the vanilla. Heat oven to 350°F. Lightly butter a 2-quart shallow baking dish. Fold the macaroni and the apples together and spread in bottom of the baking dish. Carefully pour in the custard mixture. Sprinkle top with nutmeg. Set the dish in a larger baking pan and add 1 inch of hot water. Bake until set, about 55 minutes.

Pastina with Maple Syrup and Dates

3 cups milk
1/2 cup pastina
1/4 cup maple syrup
2 tablespoons butter, softened
1/4 cup chopped pitted dates
1/2 teaspoon vanilla extract

Scald milk in a medium saucepan. Stir in the pastina and cook, stirring frequently, adjusting heat to prevent scorching, until pastina is tender and the mixture is thickened, about 20 minutes. Add the maple syrup, butter, dates, and vanilla. Spoon into small custard cups and cool slightly before serving.

INDIAN-STYLE SWEET NOODLES

1 half load of pasta dough sweetened with 2
tablespoons of sugar and made
into 3" oriental noodles
1/2 cup butter or margarine
1 cup almonds, cashews, or macadamia nuts
1 cup golden raisins **OR** *dried currants, plumped*
in hot water for about 20 minutes, then drained
2 quarts unsweetened coconut milk(see note)
1-1/4 cups sugar, or to taste
1/2 teaspoon ground cardamom
4 teaspoons rose water, or to taste
fresh mint sprigs for garnish

Make oriental noodles and set aside. In a saucepan, melt the butter over medium heat. Add the nuts and sauté until lightly browned and fragrant, about 4 minutes. Stir in the raisins and sauté about 1 minute longer. Using a slotted utensil, transfer the nuts and raisins to a small bowl and set aside. Add the oriental noodles to the hot butter and cook, turning continuously, until golden, about 1 minute. Stir in the coconut milk, sugar, and cardamom and bring to a boil. Reduce the heat to low and simmer until the noodles are al dente. Stir in the rose water, nuts and raisins. Continue to simmer until the noodles are a little more tender, about 3 minutes. Serve warm in shallow bowls and garnish with mint sprigs.

NOTE: Unsweetened canned coconut milk is available in Asian markets and the ethnic sections of some supermarkets; the best is imported from Thailand. Be sure not to use the very sweet canned cream of coconut sold for tropical drinks. To make your own coconut milk, cover 4 cups shredded fresh coconut or dried unsweetened grated coconut (available in natural foods stores) with 6 cups boiling water or warmed milk and let stand for 30 minutes. Strain the liquid through cheesecloth, squeezing the cloth to extract all the liquid.

CHOCOLATE AND COCONUT ROTINI PUDDING

1 half load of pasta dough made into 1/2" rotini
4 cups milk
1/3 cup flaked coconut
1/2 cup orzo
1/2 teaspoon vanilla extract
1 cup semisweet chocolate chips
1/4 cup packed light brown sugar
pinch of salt
heavy cream

Make rotini and set aside. In a large heavy saucepan, scald the milk. Gradually stir in the rotini and cool, stirring frequently and adjusting the heat to prevent milk from boiling over and scorching, until mixture is thickened and the orzo is al dente, about 20 to 25 minutes. Stir in the sugar until dissolved. Add the chocolate and the coconut. Remove from heat and stir until the chocolate is melted. Add the vanilla and salt. Let cool at room temperature. Serve in dessert bowls with cold heavy cream drizzled on top.

Orzo Lemon and Custard Pudding

4 cups milk
2 tablespoons raisins
1/3 cup sugar
1/2 teaspoon grated lemon zest
1/2 cup orzo
1/2 teaspoon vanilla extract
1 large egg, beaten
grated nutmeg

In a large heavy saucepan, scald the milk and sugar over medium-low heat. Stir in the orzo and cook, stirring frequently and adjusting heat to prevent milk from boiling over and scorching, until mixture is thickened and orzo is al dente, about 20 to 25 minutes. Meanwhile, beat the egg in a medium bowl. Stir the raisins, lemon zest, and vanilla into the pudding until blended. Gradually add the hot pudding to the beaten egg, stirring constantly with a spoon so that egg doesn't curdle. Sprinkle with nutmeg. Cool slightly at room temperature. Serve warm. Pudding will thicken and set upon cooling.

APPLE LASAGNE

1 half load of pasta dough made into lasagne
1-1/4 cups milk
1 egg
1 egg yolk
1 tablespoon cornstarch
1 tablespoon powdered sugar
1-3/4 pounds cooking apples
2 tablespoons butter
1/3 cup powdered sugar
1/4 cup raisins
1/2 teaspoon apple pie spice
1/4 cup walnuts, finely chopped
powdered sugar, if desired
whipped cream, if desired

Make lasagne, cook al dente, drain, rinse and set aside. In a medium-size saucepan, heat milk. In a medium-size bowl, mix together egg, egg yolk, cornstarch and 1 tablespoon powdered sugar. Pour hot milk into egg mixture while stirring. Return to saucepan. Cook over medium-low heat, stirring constantly, until thickened. Set aside. Peel, core and slice apples. Put into a medium saucepan with butter, 1/3 cup powdered sugar and a little water. Cook 10 minutes or until apples are soft. Stir in raisins and apple pie spice. Preheat oven to 375°F. In a buttered baking dish, layer lasagne and apple mixture, ending with an apple layer. Pour custard over apples. Sprinkle with walnuts. Bake 25 minutes or until set. Decorate with powdered sugar and serve with a dollop of whipped cream, if desired.

POPPYSEED PAPPARDELLE WITH BUTTERSCOTCH APPLES

*1 full load of Sweet Poppyseed Pasta
made into pappardelle (recipe follows)*

BUTTERSCOTCH APPLES
*1/2 cup butter or margarine
5 large apples, peeled, cored, and thinly sliced
2 teaspoons ground cinnamon
1 cup chopped pecans OR walnuts
3 tablespoons poppy seeds
1/2 cup dried currants OR raisins, plumped in
cognac or hot water for 20 minutes, then drained
1 cup heavy (whipping) cream OR half-and-half
1 cup packed light brown sugar*

Make pappardelle and set aside. To make the Butterscotch Apples, melt the butter in a sauté pan or skillet over medium heat. Add the apple slices, cinnamon, nuts, poppy seeds, and drained currants or raisins and sauté until the apples are lightly browned. In a saucepan, combine the cream or half-and-half and the brown sugar over low heat and simmer, stirring, until the brown sugar is completely dissolved about 4 to 5 minutes. Pour over the apples and simmer until the apples are tender but still hold their shape and the cream is slightly thickened. Meanwhile, cook pasta until al dente, drain and transfer to a heated bowl. Pour the Butterscotch Apples over the pasta and gently toss to coat well. To serve, spoon into preheated bowls and serve immediately.

SWEET POPPYSEED PASTA

2 pasta measuring cups of all-purpose flour
3 eggs, room temperature
1 teaspoon olive oil
1/4 teaspoon salt (optional)
1/3 cup poppyseed
1/2 cup powdered sugar

Follow the instructions for making pasta in your Automatic Pasta Maker Instruction booklet.

ORZO SAUCEPAN PUDDING

3-1/2 cups milk
1/2 cup orzo
1/3 cup sugar
1/2 teaspoon vanilla extract

Combine the milk and sugar in a small heavy saucepan. Scald milk, stirring, over medium-low heat. Stir in the orzo. Cook, stirring frequently and adjusting heat to prevent milk from boiling over and scorching, until the mixture is very thick and orzo is tender to the bite, 20 to 25 minutes. Remove from heat and stir in the vanilla. Pour mixture into a large bowl or four individual custard cups. Cool slightly. Serve warm or at room temperature for dessert or breakfast and top with chilled heavy cream if desired.

VARIATIONS: The flavor in this pudding are easily changed by adding grated lemon or orange zest; using lemon extract instead of vanilla;or by adding 2 tablespoons raisins, dried currants, or minced candied orange or minced dried apricots.

APRICOT PUDDING

1 half load of pasta dough made into tagliatelle
4 ounces dried apricots
1 cup warm water
cinnamon stick
2 tablespoons fresh orange juice
2 teaspoons finely grated orange rind
1/2 cup brown sugar
2 teaspoons arrowroot blended with
2 teaspoons water
1 ounce bread crumbs, made from stale bread
1/4 cup ground walnuts
1/2 cup butter or margarine, melted

Place apricots in a bowl, pour warm water over and set aside to soak for 1 hour. Drain apricots and reserve liquid. Place apricots, 2 tablespoons reserved liquid, cinnamon stick, orange juice, orange rind and 1 tablespoon brown sugar in a saucepan. Bring to a boil, then reduce heat, cover and simmer for 10 to 15 minutes or until apricots are tender. Stir arrowroot mixture into apricot mixture and cook for 2 to 3 minutes longer or until mixture thickens. Remove pan from heat and set aside to cool. Cook tagliatelle until al dente, drain and set aside. Coat a buttered 8-inch souffle dish with bread crumbs. Place one-third tagliatelle in base of soufle dish and top with half apricot mixture. Repeat layers, sprinkle with walnuts and remaining sugar, and top with remaining tagliatelle. Pour butter over pudding and bake for 25 minutes at 375°F. Turn onto a plate and cut into wedges to serve.

SWEET-CHEESE RAVIOLI WITH CHOCOLATE SAUCE

1 full load of pasta dough made into ravioli

SWEET-CHEESE FILLING
*1 pound mascarpone OR cream cheese,
at room temperature
3 tablespoons sugar, or to taste
2 egg yolks*

CHOCOLATE SAUCE
*8 ounces semisweet chocolate, chopped
2 tablespoons butter or margarine
1 cup whipping cream
1 teaspoon vanilla extract
1 egg, lightly beaten
3 tablespoons butter or margarine, melted
multicolored confectioner's sprinkles for garnish*

To make the filling, combine the cheese, sugar, and egg yolk in a bowl. Set aside. To make the sauce, combine the chocolate, butter, and cream in a saucepan or double-boiler over low heat. Cook, stirring frequently, until the chocolate is melted and the mixture is smooth. Stir in the vanilla and cool to room temperature. Set aside. Slowly reheat just before serving. Make ravioli according to the instructions in the Making Pasta chapter filling them with the sweet-cheese filling. You'll need to make 5-inch squares rolled out as thin as possible. Mound about 3 tablespoons of the filling in the center of half of the squares. Brush the exposed dough around the filling with the beaten

egg. Cover each with the remaining pasta squares
and press around the filling to eliminate air and
seal. Cut with cookie cutters into fanciful shapes,
or trim edges with a fluted pastry wheel. Cook
ravioli, a few at a time, until al dente. Using a slotted utensil, remove the ravioli to a platter. Lightly
brush with the melted butter. To serve, ladle a
pool of the reheated sauce onto preheated plates,
top with a ravioli, and sprinkle with multi-colored
sprinkles. Serve immediately.

VARIATION: For a change try making this recipe
using colored, peppermint-flavored pasta (see
recipe below).

PEPPERMINT PASTA

2 pasta measuring cups of all-purpose flour
3 eggs, room temperature
1 teaspoon olive oil
1/4 teaspoon salt (optional)
several drops of peppermint oil or to taste
1/2 cup powdered sugar
red or bright pink food color paste (optional)

Follow the instructions for making pasta in your
Automatic Pasta Maker Instruction booklet.

Glossary

Chapter 15

Agnolotti
The name means "fat little lambs," but agnolotti look more like plump semicircular ravioli. Typically filled with spinach and cheese. (see Ravioli).

Al Dente
The Italian term used to describe the texture of pasta which is perfectly cooked: tender but not soft, with a bit of bite or resistance. See Cooking Pasta, Page 30.

Angel Hair Pasta
Also labeled as capelli di angelo this is an extremely long thin pasta, that is dried in coils to prevent it from breaking. Because of its delicate nature angel's hair pasta is best served with a light sauce.

Arugula
A green leafy vegetable sometimes used in place of spinach or watercress in stuffed pasta.

Basil
Fragrant, full-flavored herb with large, bright green, tender leaves. The leaves bruise easily, losing texture and some of their flavor in chopping, so they are best shredded using scissors. The flavor of basil diminishes on cooking, so it is usually added late in the preparation of a dish. The flavor of dried basil does not compare well with that of the fresh herb so it is best avoided in this form. Buy growing pots or plant a large potful outside in summer months. Use any excess for making pesto.

255

Bay Leaves

An evergreen shrub of the laurel family, the leaves have a distinct flavor which is excellent in many savory dishes and some sweet puddings. Bay leaves also freeze well and the herb may be dried.

Bean Sprouts

These are sprouted mung beans, harvested when the shoots are about 1 to 2 inches long and still white. They are crunchy and delicately flavored, and may be used raw or very lightly cooked in a wide range of dishes including chow mein. Mung beans may be sprouted by first soaking overnight in cold water, then draining and keeping moist in a part-covered jam jar for 2 to 3 days. The beans must be rinsed with water every day and kept in a warm place so that they germinate. The jar may be covered with a piece of white cotton, kept in place with an elastic band.

Bows or Fiochetti

You can make these by hand, by cutting small circles of thinly rolled pasta and pinching or twisting each one in the middle.

Butterflies or Farfalle

This pasta is ideal for serving with meat and vegetable sauces because the sauce becomes trapped in the folds. You can make these by hand by cutting small squares of thinly rolled pasta and pinching or twisting each one in the middle.

Cannelloni

Dried cannelloni are wide tubes about 4 inches long. Fresh cannelloni are made by cutting sheets of pasta and rolling them around the filling. This large hollow pasta is most often stuffed, topped with a sauce and cheese, then baked. Cannelloni can also be stuffed and deep-fried until crisp. If deep-frying, the tubes will need to be boiled before stuffing and frying. Lasagne sheets can also be used for baked cannelloni by spreading the filling down the center of the lasagne then rolling up.

Cappelletti

Circles of pasta dough stuffed with a filling and folded to look like a pointed hat.

Cardamom

An aromatic, mild spice. The small pale green pods consist of a papery covering which conceals compartments filled with small black seeds. The whole pods are added to dishes and they may be chewed. They have a refreshing, zesty, lemon-ginger flavor which is used in both savory and sweet cooking.

Chick Peas

Small round dried pulses, also known as Garbonzo beans, pale cream in color with indented sides. When dried, they require soaking overnight before boiling in water for about 50 minutes, or until tender. Canned chick peas have an excellent texture. Their nutty flavor is good with pasta and their high protein content is valuable in main dishes.

Cavatelli
Medium-size shells with ruffled edges. A good shape for holding dressing and diced ingredients.

Chilies
There are many types of chilies, varying in hotness, from extremely fiery types to mild chilies. The small, wiry chilies are often very hot; canned jalapeño chilies are fairly mild. As well as heat, chilies have a distinct peppery flavor which is most apparent in the milder types. The seeds are especially hot, so cut out the core and rinse away all seeds before use. Always wash your hands after handling chilies as their juices are highly irritating, causing an excruciating, burning sensation when it comes in contact with sensitive areas, such as eyes, or any grazed skin or cuts.

Chinese Dried Mushrooms
Although several types of dried fungus are used in Chinese cooking, this term refers to dried shitake mushrooms. The cap, which varies in size from 1 to 3 inches, is dark outside and the stalks are usually very woody. They have a slightly musty flavor which adds a rich, distinctive characteristic taste to oriental dishes. These mushrooms must be soaked for at least 15 minutes, then drained and the stalks removed before cooking. The soaking liquor is often kept and used to flavor sauces.

Chinese Egg Noodles
Fine round noodles made from a rich egg dough. Available fresh from oriental supermarkets, these

freeze extremely well. The noodles cook in 1 to 2 minutes in boiling water, slightly longer if frozen.

Chives
Herb which resembles fine round grass, this has an onion-like flavor. Snip into very short lengths using scissors instead of chopping.

Cilantro Leaves
Fresh herb grown from coriander seeds, this resembles flat-leafed parsley in appearance but it has a strong flavor.

Cinnamon
Sweet spice used in savory and sweet cooking. Obtained from the bark of a tree, cinnamon is sold as sticks, which is the rolled bark stripped of the rough outer covering, or ground. Cinnamon is also available as rough pieces of unstripped bark. Sticks and bark are removed from dishes before eating.

Coconut Milk
Made by soaking coconut flesh in boiling water, then draining and squeezing out all the liquid. Fresh or unsweetened, shredded coconut may be used. However, it is easier to buy instant coconut milk in powder form. Creamed coconut, sold as blocks or in cans, may also be melted or diluted in hot water to make coconut milk. Instant powder is most convenient and it has the longest shelf life before the package is opened.

259

Conchigli
Stuffed seashell-shaped pasta.

Coriander
Aromatic spice with mild flavor. Small, round, pale seeds about the size of peppercorns which may be crushed. Ready ground types are also available.

Crimini Mushrooms
Crimini mushrooms are medium in size with closed caps which are brown rather than beige in color. They have a slightly stronger flavor than regular button or closed cap mushrooms. See mushrooms.

Croutons
Small cubes or shapes of fried bread, used as a garnish or to add a contrast in texture to dishes.

Cumin
Small, slim, oval seeds with a distinct flavor; usually white, although black seeds are also available. Ground cumin has a strong flavor.

Curry Powder
A mixture of spices, including fenugreek, coriander, cumin, cinnamon, chili powder, turmeric and cloves. Curry powder is a British invention to use instead of mixing individual spices to achieve a specific flavor in a dish, which is authentic to Indian cooking.

Dates
Fresh dates have firm flesh and a papery skin which is easily rubbed or peeled off. Halve the dates or slit them down one side to remove the pits. Delicious when sliced and tossed with crumbled goat's cheese and pasta.

Dill
Feathery herb which resembles fennel in appearance but has a delicate, distinctive flavor which is excellent with seafood or eggs. Dried dill is not recommended. Freeze fresh dill and use frozen in sauces.

Dim Sum
Chinese snacks, including little ravioli-like pastas filled with a variety of sweet, meaty, or other flavor, made from a pasta-like dough.

Dolcelatte
A creamy blue cheese of the Gorgonzola family but far milder. Delicious with pasta, either gently melted into warm cream to make a rich sauce or diced and tossed with hot, buttery pasta.

Dried Mushrooms
Boletus or cep (or porcini in Italian) are available dried in slices or smaller pieces. They are soaked before use and the soaking water should be retained to flavor sauces. There are other types of dried mushroom to be found in delicatessens, some strung up whole. They have a strong flavor, so are used in small quantities.

261

Fettuccine
A flat ribbon pasta that is used in a similar way to spaghetti. Often sold coiled in nests, fettuccine is particularly good with creamy sauces, which cling better than heavier sauces.

Flageolet Beans
Small, oval, pale green pulses. They have a delicate flavor which goes well with pasta. Buy dried and soak overnight, then boil them for about 45 minutes or use canned. Excellent with lamb, mint and pasta.

Fusilli
Thin round pasta coiled like a spring.

Ginger root (fresh)
Knobby root with a beige color. When young, the skin is thin and the flesh zesty and tender. Older ginger root which is tough, wrinkled, and softened is not worth buying. The flavor is slightly lemony and slightly hot–but large quantities of fresh ginger root have to be used before a hot flavor is imparted to a dish.

Gnocchi
A type of pasta made from soft dough shaped into small pieces and boiled. Semolina or potato may be used as the base or a dough of ricotta cheese and spinach may be shaped into gnocchi.

Kasha
Made from roasted buckwheat, this granular cereal can be cooked like rice and has a pleasant, nutty flavor. It is very high in protein and is wheat-free and gluten-free.

Lasagne
Wide strips or squares of pasta. These flat sheets of pasta are most often layered with a meat, fish or vegetable sauce, topped with cheese, then baked to make a delicious and satisfying dish.

Linguine
This long thin pasta is similar to spaghetti but has squarecut ends. It may be used in recipes that call for spaghetti, fettuccine or tagliatelle.

Mace
Spice which forms a netlike covering around the nutmeg. It is available dried in orange-colored pieces, known as blades, or ground. Excellent with duck, game, meat and sausage meat dishes.

Macaroni
Short-cut or 'elbow' macaroni, very common outside of Italy, is most often used in baked dishes and in the ever-popular macaroni and cheese.

Marjoram
Sweet herb with distinct flavor that is typical of Mediterranean dishes. It may be used fresh or dried; fresh, it has a mild flavor.

Mint
Familiar herb which is best when fresh or frozen.

Mozzarella Cheese
Small round unripened cheeses with a rubbery texture and delicious creamy mild flavor. Traditionally made from buffalo milk. Italian mozzarella is recommended for its superior flavor. Used in salads, as a pizza topping and for baking on pasta dishes.

Mushrooms
There are many types of edible mushrooms; however, the familiar fresh mushrooms also vary. Button mushrooms that are very small are ideal for cooking whole or halved. They are pale and mild in flavor. Slightly larger button mushrooms which are nominally darker in color are ideal for slicing. Field mushrooms or large open cap mushrooms are dark with large caps. They may be stuffed or broiled, or sliced for using in a dark sauce as they have a good flavor. However they will discolor a pale sauce. Crimini mushrooms are medium in size with closed caps which are brown rather than beige in color. They have a slightly stronger flavor than regular button or closed cap mushrooms. Specialty varieties include oyster mushrooms which are soft, pale and delicate. They are large flat, fan-shaped caps which are delicate in appearance and flavor. They should be cooked briefly, by poaching or sauteing. They are ideal in a mixed mushroom dish.

Nutmeg

Hard, round nut which is grated on a small grater. The spice has a sweet, strong flavor which is valued in savory and sweet cooking. Good with cheese and in milk sauces.

Olive Oil

An essential adjunct to fresh Italian pasta. Whole books have been devoted to olive oil as there is so much to say about the production and quality of the ingredient. In brief, oils vary significantly: dark green extra virgin olive oil is taken from the first pressing of the olives. It has a rich flavor which is delicious with garlic and Parmesan cheese to dress fresh pasta. Lighter colored oil which is taken from successive pressings has less flavor. Most supermarkets offer a range of qualities. Price and color are a good indication of flavor, and superior varieties are sold in some delicatessens. It is worth buying a small bottle of rich olive oil if you like the flavor. Smell the oil and you will notice the difference before you taste the sweetness in its flavor. Average quality olive oil is fine for cooking. Look for a mixture of olive and sunflower oil if you find the flavor of olive oil alone too strong.

Orecchiette

Its name means 'little ears' and that's what this pasta looks like. It is made without eggs and has a firm, chewy texture. Traditionally made at home, it can now be bought dried from some supermarkets.

Oregano
This strongly flavored herb (wild marjoram) is good with most pasta dishes. It may be used dried as well as fresh.

Orzo
This small pasta is shaped like grains of rice. It can be purchased dry at most supermarkets.

Pancetta
This rich Italian ham is similar to Black Forest ham and is used for flavor in many Italian recipes.

Paglia e Fieno
This popular combination of spinach (verdi) and white noodles means hay and straw in English.

Pappardelle
This very wide ribbon pasta was traditionally served with a sauce made of rabbit, herbs and wine, but today it is teamed with any rich sauce.

Parmesan Cheese
Strong hard cheese which should be bought in a chunk, then grated as required. Or, you may process chunks of Parmesan in a food processor until fine, then freeze and use as required. Fresh Parmesan has a sweet flavor which cannot be compared with the strong odor and tang of dry grated Parmesan.

Pasta Shapes (fresh)

There is a good variety of manufactured (extruded) shapes available for fresh pasta made with the Automatic Pasta Machine, including spirals, shells, and penne as well as the usual spaghetti, linguine and fettuccini. Make your own unorthodox alternatives by cutting rolled pasta dough into small squares or shredding it into oblong pieces. See the Making Pasta chapter.

Pastina

Tiny star-shaped pasta available dry in most supermarkets. It's often used in soups or desserts.

Penne

Or quills, these are short, tubular pasta, similar to macaroni, but with ends cut at an angle rather than straight. It is particularly suited to being served with meat and heavier sauces, which catch in the hollows.

Peppercorns

Dried peppercorns are available as usually black or sometimes white, both of which give a much better flavor when freshly ground. Dried green peppercorns are lighter and easily crushed. Red or pink peppercorns are similar in size but they are not of the same family. Pickled green peppercorns are available packed in brine. Fresh green peppercorns are also available occasionally, sold on their stalks. They have a strong but refreshing pepper flavor.

Pine Nuts
Small oval, pale cream-colored seeds which have a nutty flavor. They are used plain, for example in pesto, or may be used in a variety of sauces or dishes.

Pistachio Oil
Bright green oil from pistachio nuts, this has a strong flavor and should be used sparingly.

Radiatore
Rippled, short pasta shapes that look something like radiators or accordions. They hold sauce well.

Ramekin
Small, shallow ceramic baking dish usually used to prepare individual servings.

Ravioli
Round or square shapes of stuffed pasta, depending on the region of origin.

Rice Sticks
Traditional Chinese and Japanese pasta made from rice flour. They are white in color and may be transparent. Widths range from wide ribbon noodles to very fine vermicelli. They cook quickly and have a very light flavor and texture. Available fresh from oriental supermarkets.

Ricotta Cheese
A light, soft cheese which differs from other cheeses in that it is made from the whey rather than the curds. It does not melt and run during cooking. Used in fillings for pasta and in gnocchi dough.

Rosemary
Strongly flavored herb with short, dark-green spikes which sprout along woody stems. Dried rosemary has a woody texture. Good with pork and lamb.

Sage
Herb with soft, pale-green leaves and a peppery flavor. Good with pork, vegetables and cheese.

Salsa
A Mexican term for a spicy fresh sauce.

Shells
Pasta shaped like conch shells (conchiglie). Available in small, medium and large sizes. Good for holding dressing and diced ingredients. Often used with seafood.

Spaghetti
Deriving its name from the Italian word spago meaning 'string', spaghetti is the most popular and best known of all pastas outside of Italy. It can be served with only butter or oil and is good with almost any sauce. Fresh spaghetti is sold folded in packages.

Spirals
Also called fusilli or rotini, these are among the most common fresh pasta shapes. Best served with chunky meat sauces, as the chunks are held by the coils or twists. Available in different colors.

Sun-dried Tomatoes
Available in packages, the tomatoes are easily shredded with scissors. They impart a rich flavor to dishes. Soak them in liquid or olive oil to soften (some are packed in olive oil) or simmer in sauce.

Tagliatelle
Another of the flat ribbon pastas, tagliatelle is eaten more in northern Italy than in the south and is used in the same ways as fettuccine.

Tahini
A beige-colored paste made from sesame seeds.

Thyme
Familiar, small-leafed herb with a strong flavor. Use fresh or dried.

Tofu
Also known as bean curd, this is prepared from soya beans. It is sold in blocks, displayed in the refrigerated section. The natural curd is tasteless and it readily absorbs the flavor of other ingredients cooked with it. Smoked and flavored Tofu are also available.

Tortellini
Small stuffed pasta shapes enclosing a little filling. They are shaped by stuffing squares or rounds of pasta and sealing in a triangular shape, then pinching long ends together.

Turmeric
Bright yellow spice ground from a root of the same color. It has a distinct mild flavor.

Wagon wheels
Medium-size wheel shapes. Also called ruote, or rotelie.

Walnut Oil
Strongly flavored oil which should be used sparingly as a flavoring rather than for frying. It can also be used to add a nutty flavor to pasta dough or added to sauces.

Won Tons
Small Chinese dumplings made from a light pasta-like dough with a small amount of filling. These dumplings may be simmered in water or stock or can be deep-fried.

Ziti
Medium-size pasta tubes with straight-cut edges.